THE INTELLIGENT NETWORK

Prentice Hall Series In
Advanced Communications Technologies

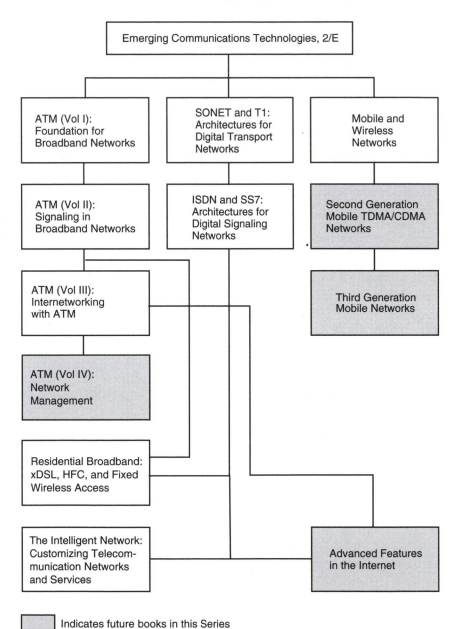

Emerging Communications Technologies, 2/E

ATM (Vol I):
Foundation for
Broadband Networks

SONET and T1:
Architectures for
Digital Transport
Networks

Mobile and
Wireless
Networks

ATM (Vol II):
Signaling in
Broadband Networks

ISDN and SS7:
Architectures for
Digital Signaling
Networks

Second Generation
Mobile TDMA/CDMA
Networks

ATM (Vol III):
Internetworking
with ATM

Third Generation
Mobile Networks

ATM (Vol IV):
Network
Management

Residential Broadband:
xDSL, HFC, and Fixed
Wireless Access

The Intelligent Network:
Customizing Telecom-
munication Networks
and Services

Advanced Features
in the Internet

Indicates future books in this Series

THE INTELLIGENT NETWORK
CUSTOMIZING TELECOMMUNICATION NETWORKS AND SERVICES

UYLESS BLACK

Prentice Hall PTR
Upper Saddle River, New Jersey 07458
http://www.phptr.com

Library of Congress Cataloging-in-Publication Data

Black, Uyless D.
   The intelligent network / Uyless Black.
      p.   cm.
   Includes bibliographical references and index.
   ISBN 0-13-793019-4
   1. Telecommunication systems. 2. Telecommunication—Switching
systems. I. Title.
TK5101.B5528 1998
621.385—dc21   97-47329
                                                                                      CIP

Aquisitions editor: Mary Franz
Cover designer: Scott Weiss
Cover design director: Jerry Votta
Manufacturing manager: Alexis R. Heydt
Marketing manager: Miles Williams
Compositor/Production services: Pine Tree Composition, Inc.

Published by Prentice Hall PTR
Prentice-Hall, Inc.
A Simon & Schuster Company
Upper Saddle River, New Jersey 07458

Prentice Hall books are widely used by corporations and government agencies
for training, marketing, and resale.

The publisher offers discounts on this book when ordered in bulk quantities. For
more information contact:

          Corporate Sales Department
          Phone: 800-382-3419
          Fax: 201-236-7141
          E-mail: corpsales@prenhall.com

          Or write:

          Prentice Hall PTR
          Corp. Sales Dept.
          One Lake Street
          Upper Saddle River, New Jersey 07458

Printed in the United States of America
10 9 8 7 6 5 4 3 2 1

ISBN: 0-13-793019-4

Prentice-Hall International (UK) Limited, *London*
Prentice-Hall of Australia Pty. Limited, *Sydney*
Prentice-Hall Canada Inc., *Toronto*
Prentice-Hall Hispanoamericana, S.A., *Mexico*
Prentice-Hall of India Private Limited, *New Delhi*
Prentice-Hall of Japan, Inc., *Tokyo*
Simon & Schuster Asia Pte. Ltd., *Singapore*
Editora Prentice-Hall do Brasil, Ltda., *Rio de Janeiro*

This book on intelligent networks is dedicated to a scientist named Konrad Lorenz, a gifted Nobel prize winner who has written extensively about intelligence and social behavior. In these times it is a good idea to reflect upon a thought from Lorenz, who penned these words in his classic book, *On Aggression:*

> The [man/woman] who behaves socially from natural inclination normally makes few demands on the controlling mechanism of [his/her] own moral responsibility.

Those thoughts seem to have been forgotten or ignored by many people today.

This book deals with the intelligent network (IN), a term coined in Europe to describe a computer-based network with sophisticated capabilities. Not to be outdone, the Americans coined the term advanced intelligent network (AIN), to describe the same type of network.

Some people may take issue with classifying these networks as intelligent, and the very term "intelligent" can be confusing to those who think these networks deal with the discipline called artificial intelligence (AI). The networks described in this book do not deal with AI, and AI engineers would likely state that the term intelligent is not really indicative of the functions of the technology.

Maybe not, but maybe so. After all, what is intelligence? Try conjuring up your own definition before reading further, and then see how your view jells with the following thoughts.

"Intelligence" is an interesting word, and a controversial subject. The word has different meanings to different people, and we humans spend a lot of time deciding what is and what is not intelligent. Here is what Webster has to say about the topic: ". . . having a good understanding or a high capacity; quick to comprehend, as persons or animals."

That definition was written before the ascendancy of the computer in our lives, and one wonders if Webster would have expanded this definition to include the computer. For my own definition, I would add the notion of intuition, and the ability to channel aggression to non-lethal behavior. I believe these traits to be fundamental to intelligence.

In some circles, it is believed the modern computer possesses intelligence, and the recent man-machine duel between an IBM computer and chess player Kasparov brought the controversy to the general public. Furthermore, noted people in the field, such as Bill Gates, state that the human brain will some day be replicated by a computer. Others state that we are reaching the point in science where we know many of the basic physical aspects of what makes up "intelligence."

Without question, we are building computers and computer networks that have remarkable capabilities, and one of the goals of an intelligent network is to *appear* to its user to be intelligent (intuitive), and to be quick to comprehend the user's needs for services, and respond to those needs. Well, so-far-so-good, but we must digress for a moment.

A large circle of people view the human as the pinnacle of intelligence and other forms of life to be either devoid of intelligence or lacking the capacity found in humans. Well, we humans have thumbs—and that aspect of our inventory helps in making tools, at which we are supreme. And the computer is ultimately—another human-made tool.

Placing the computer discussion aside for a moment, I am not sure that much of our behavior is more intelligent than other creatures on this planet, especially in how we are applying some of our tools. What I mean is that our neighboring creatures are not bent on the pathological destruction of their societies and our planet. We seem to be.

With our many tools, we have surely mastered much of the physical world around us, but we are not so good at dealing in a sensible manner with our own societies. Look around you. Who is more intelligent, the vast majority of creatures who use aggression solely to survive, or we humans who routinely use aggression to deal with problems that are considered natural conflicts in the animal world.

Is it intelligent to devastate a human culture, because the culture is different from another? Is it intelligent to garrote a neighbor because the neighbor looked the wrong way at you, or was wearing a coveted pair of sneakers?

I could go on with other examples, but the answer to my questions, . . . is of course not. Then why does our so-called intelligent species behave the way we do?

In a nutshell, it is because our society has failed to study adequately and understand the relationship of the modern and primitive aspects of our inherited behavior, and how we modern humans deal with it.

Time-and-time again almost all members of the natural world exhibit behavior toward their own species in a manner that is meant to preserve the species. Aggressive behavior is channeled. If it does occur, the creature warns its potential adversary of the same species with well-known ritualistic behavior. And the aggression may be fierce, but its intent is not to kill.

For example, take a look at the behavior of a wolf (or most any other animal, fish, or bird for that matter). The wolf has well-defined ways of positioning its ears, eyes, nose, and mouth that convey its feelings and intent. It attacks viciously only if it is cornered, hunting another species, or if it is protecting its young. And that mode of behavior pertains, with rare exceptions, to most species in the world.

But there are exceptions to this behavior. The social organization of humans, rats, bees, termites, and others are such that encountering different cultures of the same species often result in furious attacks, designed to kill the other culture. Bees and termites resort to this behavior if their turf is invaded. Humans and rats are not so selective.

Unfortunately, we tool-building humans have very efficient tools to apply against the fellow members of our species. And in what name, under what cause do we humans take up our tools against each other? Usually, aggression occurs under the names of pride and power, and under causes that rarely deal with anything but protecting pride, and expanding power for its own sake . . . but rarely the survival of life. The sobering aspect of this trend is that our tools to destruct are gradually but surely finding their way into the hands of those who don't mind the destruction of a culture if it furthers the pride and power base of another.

So, after all things considered, my vote is still out on the "lofty" pinnacle of human intelligence. Sometimes, the wolf's behavior seems preferable.

Well, on these cheerful notes, our goal in this book is considerably more modest than finding the underlying aspects of human intelligence and aggression. Our "intelligent network" in this book represents a computer-based tool that is quick to comprehend, and has a high capacity, but it is far from being intuitive. As we shall see, creating an intelligent network is simply a matter of building standardized and reusable software modules that provide network services that are common to users, and building specialized modules for unique services. The term intelligence is applied to this approach. I call it common sense.

Contents

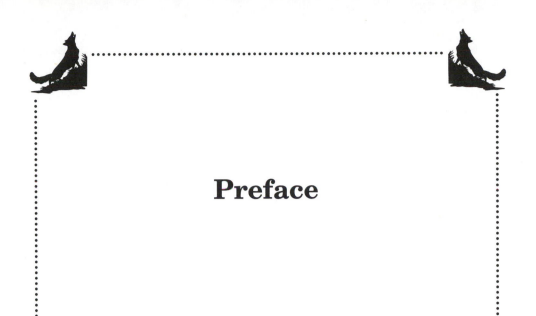

Preface

This book is one in a series titled *Advanced Communications Technologies,* and is written as a complement to this series. The focus of this book is an emerging technology, known by two names: intelligent networks or advanced intelligent networks. Both terms convey the idea of a network that provides a platform to deploy user services in a fast and efficient manner.

Most of these services are related to telephone-type features, such as a "do not disturb" application, a "call screening" application, and so on. But the architecture of this network strives to be application independent. The goal is to build a software platform that consists of programs that are reusable across applications.

Most of the work on the development of this technology is coordinated by the International Telecommunications Union—Telecommunication Standardization Sector (ITU-T) and Bellcore. Both organizations publish models on the subject. (Chapter 2 provides the references for these specifications.) The ITU-T model uses the term *intelligent network* (*IN*). The Bellcore model uses the term *advanced intelligent network* (*AIN*). This book describes the specifications that are published by these organizations, and includes tutorials on the rationale and use of the models. Nortel's ServiceBuilder is used as an example of a commercial deployment of the IN and AIN models.

The models have undergone revisions and are now published in different releases. This book emphasizes those specifications that are more prevalent in commercial products at this time, specifically the ITU-T Capability Set 1 (CS-1) and the Bellcore AIN 0.1.

The approach to explaining the models is as follows: Chapters 1, 2, and 5 discuss the two models together, since they have many common features. Chapters 3 and 7 concentrate on the ITU-T model, and Chapter 6 is devoted to the Bellcore model. Appendix D shows examples of how the Bellcore AIN is used in toll-free services.

This approach should satisfy the reader who wants a general review of the subject matter (Chapters 1, 2 and 5) as well as the reader who wants more detailed information (Chapters 3, 6, 7, and Appendix D).

Be aware that this book is meant as a pedagogical tool for the analysis of intelligent networks, and the designer must go to the specifications in order to implement a system. I hope that I have made that path an easier one by the publication of this book.

ACKNOWLEDGMENTS

The many people in the ITU-T and Bellcore working groups that have been working on the specifications for intelligent networks and advanced intelligent networks are as much a collective author of this book as I. I would like to thank them and the ITU-T and Bellcore for a significant contribution to the telecommunications industry.

The explanations and tutorials in this book about the subject matter reflect my thoughts, and should not be attributed to these individuals and organizations.

I would also like to thank Nortel for sharing with me the architecture and services of their ServiceBuilder product. Their engineers and designers have been very helpful to me during this project. Nortel also provided information on the basic call models in Chapter 5.

1

IN Introduction

This chapter introduces the basic concepts of the intelligent network (IN). The purpose of the IN is described as well as its major components. A history of the evolution of IN explains how the technology began with the automation of operator services and the implementation of toll-free numbers. Several market forecasts and vendor surveys are also included in this chapter.

IN GOALS

A fundamental aspect of the intelligent network (IN) is the ability to support the creation of services for the end customer in a rapid manner. The IN uses the technology of Signaling System Number 7 (SS7) and adds its functionality at the application layer to achieve these key goals:

- Provide timely creation of new services for the customer
- Support a wide range of services (generic and tailored)
- Support efficient maintenance of the IN system
- Require a seamless environment between vendors' systems
- Insofar as possible, automate services that entail operator intervention

This last goal has been at the top of the list with telephone service providers. In the United States alone, about 30,000 operators handle some 7 billion directory access (DA) queries each year. The average operator work time for a typical DA call is 19 to 28 seconds—most of which entails greeting the caller and obtaining the information to service the caller's request. The automation of DA calls can save telephone companies enormous sums of money. It is estimated that every second eliminated by DA automation from the manual operators' 19 to 28 second work saves the telephone industry $65 to $80 million a year.

WHAT IS AN IN SERVICE?

A frequently asked question is, "What is an IN service?" Another question that is common is, "What is an example of an IN service?" The term *IN service* is misleading, because IN is designed to be service independent. In fact, service independence is one of the key components of IN. The value of IN is that it standardizes the procedures and protocols to provide IN services to a customer in accordance with the five goals cited earlier.

The term *intelligent network (IN)* is used in the international standards, published by the ITU-T. The term *advanced intelligent network (AIN)* is used by Bellcore. This book focuses on both standards, which are similar. I use these two terms interchangeably throughout the book, since most vendors/manufacturers are implementing both standards in their products. In specific discussions, I will use the terms in the context of the standard's mentor, the ITU-T or Bellcore. On those occasions, I will clarify how I am using the terms. On a general level, I use the term IN.

MARKET PREDICTIONS

To begin our analysis of intelligent networks, it will prove helpful to examine the projected market for this technology. Numerous studies estimate the revenue gained from (IN) services for the next few years (see Figure 1–1). Several studies indicate that by the year 2000 IN services will comprise as much as 30% of telephone company revenues. In addition, revenues from mobile services will range from 25 to 33% of the total IN revenues.

Surveys have been conducted of the U.S. and European markets for IN equipment sales. Various estimates indicate that IN equipment sales

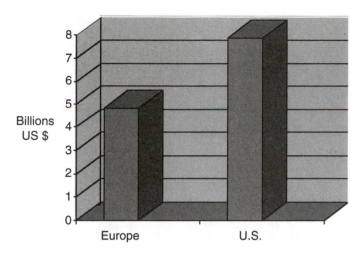

Figure 1–1   Projected revenue for IN services in 2000.
(*Source:* **Conference on Intelligent Networks, May 9, 1996, London, IBC Technical Services, Ltd.)**

will reach $7.9 billion in the United States and $4.8 billion in Europe by the year 2000. It is anticipated that as Europe deregulates its telecommunications industry, considerable competition will ensue—in a manner similar to the United States (with the 1984 divestiture [AT&T breakup] and the 1996 Telecommunications Act). Increased competition should spur the traditional service providers to provide better performance.

Looking beyond the traditional "enhanced services," such as call waiting, providers must move into new markets. Traditional telephone services are not growing much, and to survive in the marketplace, many providers are looking for new services that will meet the customers' needs and bring in revenue.

The intelligent network is viewed as a critical tool to help the service providers offer more sophisticated services. These services are in various stages of being defined, and some of them will prove to be difficult to implement. Perhaps one of the most challenging parts of IN will be the ability to handle personal mobility in mobile networks. Equally challenging will be the ability of the IN system to support number portability.

The Venture Development Corporation (*Source:* Profiting from AIN Conference, Radisson Hotel, Atlanta, GA, January 29–30, 1997, Jerome Krasner, Conference Presenter) performed a market survey of the vendor share of the world wide AIN platform for the end of year 1995. The bar graph in Figure 1–2 represents worldwide shipments of hardware, software, and middleware/connectivity software. Siemens, Nokia, Tandem

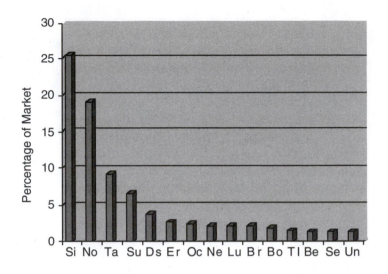

where:

Si	Siemens
No	Nokia Telecommunication
Ta	Tandem Telecom
Su	SUN Microsystems
Ds	DSC Communications
Er	Ericsson
Oc	Octel
Ne	Newbridge Networks
Lu	Lucent Technologies
Br	Brite Voice Systems
Bo	Boston Technology
TI	Texas Instruments
Be	Bellcore
Se	Sequent
Un	Unisys

Figure 1–2   Market share of AIN platform shipments (1995).

Telecom, SUN Microsystems, and DSC Communications are the early leaders in the IN marketplace, but this market is embryonic, and other companies are joining the fray. These leadership positions will likely shift during the next few years.

PRECURSORS TO IN: OSS AND 800 SERVICE

In the early days of the telephone, almost all services were provided by an operator, in this case, a person. Today, the majority of the signals and calls needed to make a connection are created by the customer.

While some services require an operator (that is to say, a real person), increasingly the operator services are being automated (that is to say, a computer). The Bell Operating Company (BOC) describes operator services systems (OSS) to include nonautomated and automated operator services. These services are divided into two major categories: *assistance,* used to assist customers in completing a call or in handling special requests, and *information (directory assistance),* used to provide telephone numbers, addressing information, and so on to the customer.

Figure 1–3 depicts a typical OSS architecture. The connections indicate that OSS has full access to end offices, tandem offices, other OSSs, databases, and operator positions. A key component of OSS is that it is designed to allow the creation of new services in a speedy manner.

The OSS consists of a tandem switching system that has special operator services. The OSS can receive calls from other local exchange carrier (LEC) and interexchange carrier (IXC) operator systems, end offices, and LEC tandems. It can route calls to these nodes. The OSS databases contain the required information for servicing calls and providing information services to customers.

OSS Features

Bellcore Document FR-NWT-000271 defines five features of OSS. Here is a brief description of these features:

Basic OSS Features. The basic OSS features include the determination of the calling number, the called number, and the billed number. To obtain these services, several operations are made available to an opera-

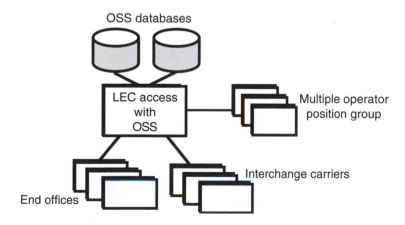

Figure 1–3 Operator Services System (OSS).

tor. First, the initial call processing operation enables the operator to determine and identify the customer-dialed signals and to receive and interpret post-seizure dialing signals. As part of this feature, a check is made to determine if the call is intraLATA or interLATA, and if the call is to be serviced by this OSS or is to be directed to an IXC. Another feature, called *sequence call processing,* is used to allow a customer to request further action during the connection. Finally, the terminating inward service allows OSSs to receive requests from each other about call completion, operator interrupt, emergency assistance, and other activities.

Customer Access Features. These features allow a customer to access an operator to obtain a variety of information, such as assistance in dialing, services offered, rates on calls, credit requests, and trouble reporting.

Customer Listing Information Features. These features allow a customer to obtain information; a listed telephone number, an address that is associated with a telephone number, and a business listing based on a trade name, business category, or geographic area.

Service Specific Call Handling Features. These features include busy line verification (determining the current status of a line), operator interrupt, teleconferencing, and recording a message that the OSS delivers to a specified station.

Special Billing Features. These features include calling card billing, calling collect, and third party billing. These services are verified through the billed number in the line information data base (LIDB).

The 800 Service

The 800 service (called Freephone or Green Number in various parts of the world) has been in existence since 1976. It was developed to provide toll-free service to telephone customers. Since that time, it has undergone several changes, primarily as the result of divestiture in 1984, the 1991 FCC requirement for number portability, and the introduction of CCS capabilities and SS7 in the late 1980s and early 1990s.

Figure 1–4 shows a typical operation for the completion of an 800 call. All calls must first be processed by a service switching point (SSP). This node recognizes the 800 number, suspends normal call processing, forms an SS7 message, and sends the message via signaling transfer

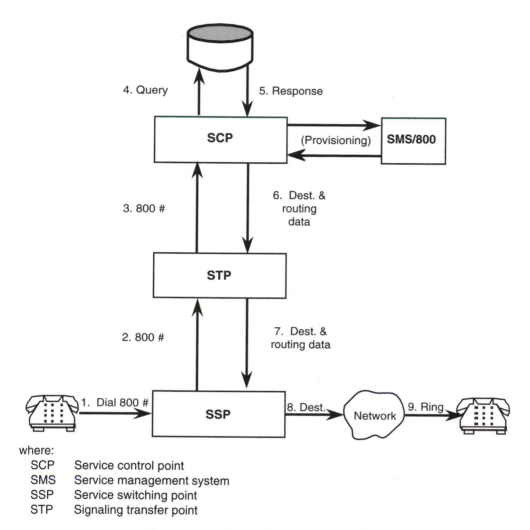

where:
SCP Service control point
SMS Service management system
SSP Service switching point
STP Signaling transfer point

Figure 1–4   The 800 database service.

point (STPs) to a service control point (SCP). The query is then sent to SCP 800 database, which contains a copy of the associated customer record. The record contents define how the call is to be handled. Based on this information, the SCP determines the carrier/POTS, based on factors such as date and time. The SCP instructs the SCP to send the call to a specified POTS or IXC. The SCP is also instructed to create a record of the call.

The service management system/800 (SMS/800) is used to provision the service. It does not participate in the actual call operations. It interacts with the customer or someone from the LEC or IXC and translates the customer's request into a standard unit of operation (call-processing logic [CPR]), and sends the CPR to the SCP.

The SCP now has sufficient information to return a message to the originating SSP (events 6 and 7). This message contains the routing data for the setting up of the call to the called party (events 8 and 9).

THE IN APPROACH

The intelligent network is an evolving concept, based on OSS and 800 operatives, and further based on the implementation of a service independent and machine independent architecture from which network service providers can create new services for the customer.

One of the key components to the success of the network and customer satisfaction with the network is the allowance and support of new services in a flexible and expeditious manner. In a nutshell, future architecture is focused on faster provisioning and customized services for the user.

A fundamental component of the IN is the ability to support the creation of services for the end customer in a rapid manner. While this goal is laudable and on the surface appears to be a simple task, it is in fact difficult and complex to achieve. The difficulty stems from the breadth of some customers' requests, and the ability to create the services to support these requests through the modification and/or addition to the network's existing hardware and software architecture. Consider that a service request may impact scores of hardware components and hundreds of software modules containing thousands of lines of code.

Therefore, service creation requires a structured and disciplined approach. It usually entails modeling, building generic blocks for simulation, and specifying the service through compiler-independent languages. In other words, it requires the development of a formal method or model.

IN SERVICE EXAMPLES

Figure 1–5 shows an example of how an IN application can be implemented to provide simple, useful services to an end user. The IN components described in general terms here, are explained in more detail in subsequent chapters. We assume that a customer wishes to order a pizza, and consults his yellow pages to find Pizza-a-Go-Go, willing and able to provide the service. In event 1, the customer dials the number

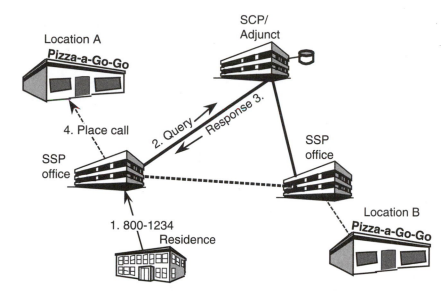

Figure 1–5   Example of an AIN service.

furnished in the yellow pages (800–1234), which is forwarded to the local central office.

This office serves as a SSP office and (under the SSP function) analyzes the number. It discovers that it must route a *query* message to another office that services this telephone number. Therefore, in event 2, the SSP office forms the IN query and sends it to an SSP/adjunct node. The calling and called addresses in this message are the SS7 destination and source point codes and the message itself is coded as a Transaction Capabilities Application Part (TCAP) message.[1]

The SCP/adjunct node uses these addresses to make a query to a database to discover the location of the nearest Pizza-a-Go-Go outlet. In event 3, it sends this information back to the SSP office. Upon receipt of this message in event 4, the SSP places a call to the pizza parlor, thus connecting the customer to the closest Pizza-a-Go-Go.

This next example is the "Do Not Disturb" service, shown in Figure 1–6. After the customer has set up the service with the IN system, whenever the customer wishes the service activated he or she dials the operator and enters a given number of predefined digits (Event 1). The SSP collects and analyzes the digits, determines that the service is IN-related (Events 2 and 3). The SSP suspends the call and sends a query

---

[1]See Appendix B for information on SS7 point codes and TCAP messages.

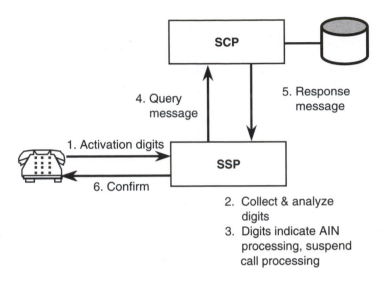

Figure 1–6   Do not disturb (activating the service).

message to the SCP (Event 4). The SCP examines the message, decodes it, and discovers that it is an activate do not disturb service for this customer. It alters the customer record to activate the service and sends back a response message to the SSP (Event 5). The SSP receives the message and signals to the customer that the service is activated with a recorded announcement (Event 6).

Once the do not disturb service is activated, calling parties may or may not be allowed to connect to the customer. Figure 1–7 illustrates how a calling party is not blocked and is allowed to connect to the customer. Once again, the SSP collects the dialed digits from the calling party and determines that the call is IN-related. As before, it suspends the call, forms the AIN message, and sends it to the SCP. The SCP examines the number and determines that the calling party is not blocked and is allowed to dial the AIN do not disturb customers. The response message to the SSP so indicates. In turn, the SSP makes the connection to the called party.

In Figure 1–8, the calling party dials the customer who subscribes to the do not disturb service, but is denied the connection, because the calling party's telephone number is not in the associated list of numbers that can be connected. In event 6, the SCP sends a message that instructs the SSP to play an announcement, collect additional digits, and act upon these digits. The SSP then sends a message to an intelligent processor (IP), and the IP plays the proper message (Events 7 and 8).

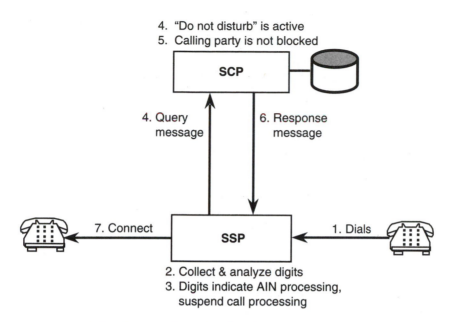

Figure 1–7   Do not disturb (allowing a call to be connected).

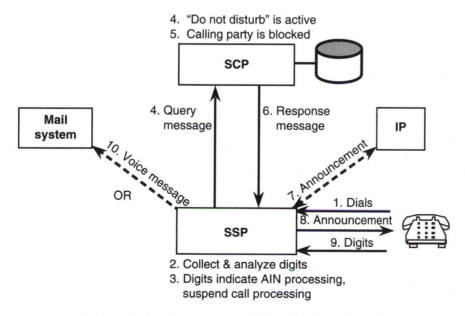

Figure 1–8   Do not disturb (disallowing the call).

As a result of the message, the calling party enters more digits (Event 9). The SSP analyzes the digits and determines that the calling party wishes to leave a message. The message is recorded by the voice mail system (Event 10). Later, the IN customer can call in and pick up this message.

These examples represent a few of the many possible features that an IN can support. The features are expanded later. For now, it should prove useful to diverge a bit, and provide more background information about the evolution of IN.

HOW IN EVOLVED

As mentioned in the first part of this chapter, there are different views in the industry about the difference between an intelligent network (IN) and an advanced intelligent network (AIN), but most people use the two terms to describe the same concept. This part of the chapter will explain how the terms came into use.

As discussed in many parts of this book, common channel signaling (CCS) partitions the signaling part of the network from the user traffic part. SS7 is the prominent CCS system in operation today.

In the early 1980s (see Figure 1–9), a switch in a telephone network contained not only: (a) switching capabilities but (b) basic call processing (BCP) and (c) database processing (the "control" or "services" data) as well. With some exceptions, all switches in the public switched network housed these three functions. In addition, the switches were built by different manufacturers, and extensive coordination was required to update the software and database contents across this heterogeneous environment. Every machine in the network had to be configured in the same way (and correctly) before anything could happen!

Of course, this all-in-one approach created duplication in the switches since they were configured with identical control databases and software. It also made change control cumbersome and complex, since multiple copies had to be maintained (at all nodes) of the data and supporting software.

To complicate matters further, during this period, each vendor had a different approach about how to handle certain tasks at a switch, which made the interworking of heterogeneous equipment a very difficult task. In addition, this monolithic approach lead to large and hard-to-change systems, which resulted in the inability to respond to the customers' requests in a timely manner. To make matters worse, any supplementary

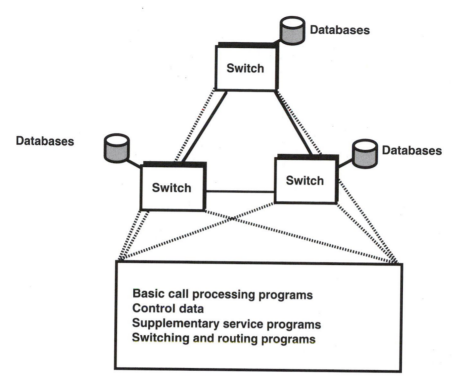

Figure 1–9   Early systems.

service was built from scratch. If a service provider decided to offer a new service, say call forwarding, software was written solely for that service. This new service also required the changing of the basic call processing modules.

As a consequence of this environment, it was hard to make timely releases to software, and even harder to build new services. It was not unusual for a new service to take two to four years to put into place.

Notwithstanding, the systems cited in the previous paragraphs provided many useful services, were effective, and generated revenue. Yet, they were cumbersome to use and maintain. Consequently as shown in Figure 1–10, the network operators decided to implement a different approach to the CCS architecture: (1) move and distribute functions into specialized modules and specialized machines, and (2) reduce the duplication of user services by placing them in one (or a few) processor(s). This approach led to the off-loading of many services and resources from the switch and permitted their being shared by a community of users. For example, in Figure 1–10, the replicated databases were centralized to the SCP.

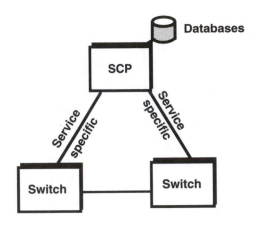

where:
  SCP   Service control point

Figure 1–10   Intelligent network architecture.

In the mid-1980s, the so-called intelligent network (IN) began to be implemented by placing services such as the 800 in the SCP. This approach represented considerable progress, but at this stage of the development, the interface (and messages) between the switch and the SCP were tailored to each service. Customized messages (noted as "service specific" in Figure 1–10) at the switch and the SCP were created for each service.

Nonetheless, this approach provided a platform from which multiple vendors could access a common resource; with the publication of SS7, it provided standardized interfaces between the vendors' equipment and software. With single (or at least fewer) copies of databases and software, it led to reduced costs and less complexity in maintenance.

A representation of the next step in the evolution towards the intelligent network is shown in Figure 1–11. The switches were responsible for basic call processing operations and the switching operations to move the signaling traffic through the network and use the signaling traffic to set up a connection.[2]

---

[2]You will notice that this figure uses the terms *switching* and *routing* to describe this process. This book will not distinguish between these two terms. Both will convey the notion of relaying information from an input port of a machine to an output port. Some people use the term switching to convey this operation being performed in hardware and the term routing as a software operation. It is not necessary to make this distinction in this book.

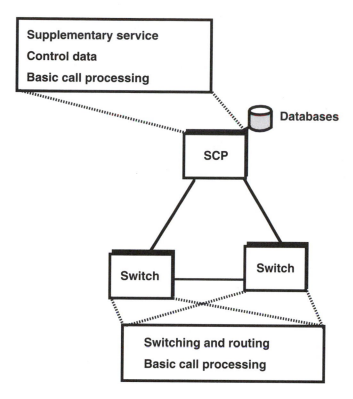

Figure 1–11   Location of components in next evolutionary step.

The supplementary service, such as 800 numbers, credit verification, and so on, are moved to the SCP. Also moved to the SCP are the databases. As mentioned earlier, this distribution of function provides a much more efficient allocation of resources in the network. However, note that in this evolutionary step, the SCP continues to perform basic call processing operations.

The effect of the modified structure is shown in Figure 1–12. I have labeled five events in Figure 1–12, with a brief legend beneath the figure to explain these events. The cogent aspect of this figure is that the switch and the SCP must execute basic call processing operations (event 2: with several messages exchanged) before the supplementary services operations can be obtained by the switch. While this approach is a noticeable improvement to other operations explained earlier in this chapter, the processes depicted in event 2 consume considerable resources in the network.

Figure 1–13 personifies the adage that necessity is the mother of invention. It makes little sense to set up connections between the switch and the SCP when, after all, the operations between these machines support a user connection, but do not form a path in the user connection. Conse-

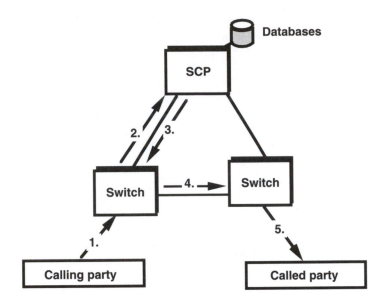

Events:
1. Dial-in to network
2. Set up connection then make request
3. Return reply
4. Set up connection
5. Set up connection

Figure 1–12   Steps in obtaining a supplementary service.

quently, the next step, as shown in Figure 1–13, is to remove the overhead involved in setting up connections between these components. Indeed, by implementing sparse, connectionless operations between the switch and the SCP, the efficiency of the operations is improved considerably.

Thus, Figure 1–13 shows a further distribution of functions and less overlap of processes. As a consequence, each machine becomes more specialized and more modular. From the standpoint of design, the actions of the machines and the software operating in those machines become more "atomic." That is, they are more independent from each other and less reliant on how their individual internal operations affect each other. Of course, the actions cannot be completely atomic, else there would be little to communicate. Later discussions revisit the concepts of atomic actions. The end result is less duplication, less complexity, and easier adaptation to changes.

Figure 1–14 shows the operations that result from the removal of basic call processing from the SCP. The differences in this scenario differ from those of Figure 1–12 with regard to events 2 and 3. Instead of establishing a connection to invoke the services of the SCP, the switch uses a

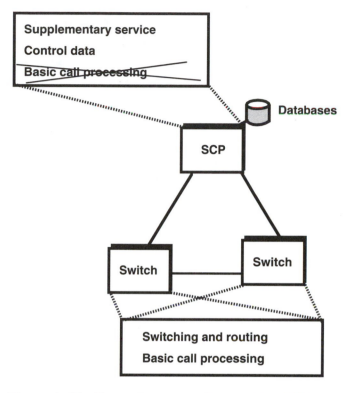

Figure 1–13   Removing connections at the SCP.

common signaling channel to obtain these same services. As we learned earlier, since events 2 and 3 occur on an out-of-band connectionless channel, the resulting operations can be done with less overhead, yielding more throughput and less delay.

Finally, as depicted in Figure 1–15, the next step in this process is called the intelligent network. Instead of tailored messages for a specific service, the IN uses a common set of standardized messages for a variety of services.[3] Thus, the switch call processing and the SCP database processing support a common interface.

---

[3]This concept is certainly not revolutionary and the software industry has been using this approach for over two decades. In an earlier phase of my career, I worked with a team of very talented programmers in the late 1970s that devised concepts entailing "code reuse" and generic software. At that time, we did not have the tools that are now available to today's programmers, notably OSI's presentation layer. Nonetheless, we developed systems for the U.S. Federal Reserve System that are similar to the concepts discussed in this chapter. In the late 1980s, the telephone industry began to use these concepts as well. The publication and acceptance of SS7 in 1984 at last provided a common (and powerful) platform to implement these concepts in the telephone network.

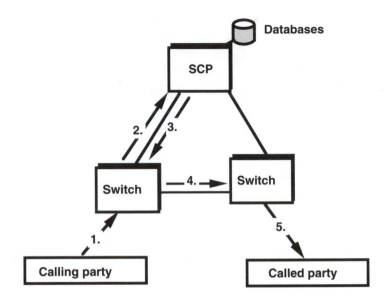

Events:
1. Dial-in to network
2. Make request on a common signaling channel
3. Return reply on a common signaling channel
4. Set up connection
5. Set up connection

Figure 1–14   Service request without a connection.

IN GOES FURTHER

IN is much more than just a set of standardized messages between SSPs and SCPs. IN is published as a standard by the ITU-T and Bellcore and contains an extensive set of rules and procedures stipulating how the information is exchanged between the IN components. In addition, the IN defines several other components that may be employed in the network. Subsequent parts of this book describe these components.

SS7 AND THE IN

Figure 1–16 shows the elements that exist today for the intelligent network. It is evident that they rest on SS7 architecture, and we have explained some of their functions in this chapter. The SCP continues to fill the role we described earlier. The switch is now divided into two func-

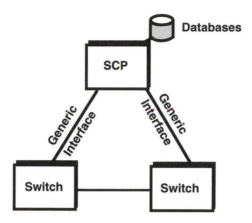

Figure 1–15   Architecture for the advanced intelligent network.

tions: the service switching point (SSP) and the signaling transfer point (STP).

The SSP is the interface to the called and calling parties labeled in this figure as "subscriber." This switch interprets the called party address (the dialed number) and determines what actions are to be taken. If the actions require the services of the SCP, a request message is created at the SSP and forwarded to the SCP through the backbone signaling network (which is supported by switches, signaling transfer points [STP]).

Therefore, the underlying architecture for the intelligent network consists of three types of machines shown in this figure: the SSP, the STP, and the SCP. These three functions could very well be implemented in one hardware architecture with different software modules. And, indeed, this is the case in many situations. Likewise, one machine may perform one or two or three of these functions. The actual physical implementation of these entities depends on the operating environment of the network.

IN MILESTONES AND WHAT'S NEXT

The IN concept and its position in the network today reflects an evolution that began in the 1960s when the concept of stored program control (SPC) was brought to the telephone switch (see Figure 1–17). With the introduction of software in the operations, the stage was set for the

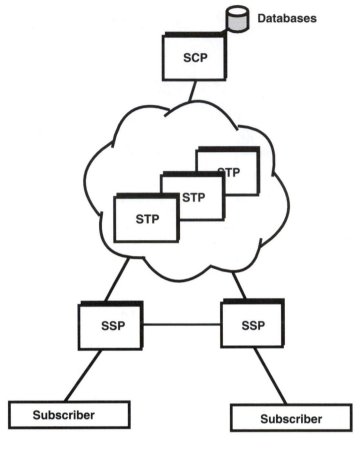

where:
SCP   Service control point
SSP   Service switching point
STP   Signaling transfer point

Figure 1–16   Elements of the intelligent network.

development of more capabilities. The use of software opened a vista for the tailoring of services to the customer.

Common channel signaling (CCS) systems were designed in the 1950s and 1960s for analog networks and later adapted for digital telephone switches. In 1976, AT&T implemented the Common Channel Interoffice Signaling (CCIS) into its toll network. This system is referred to as CCS6 and was based on the CCITT Signaling System No. 6 Recommendation. SS6 and CCS6 were slow and designed to work on low-bit-rate channels. Moreover, these architectures were not layered, which made changing the code a complex and expensive task.

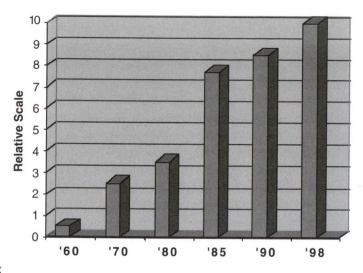

Milestones:
- '60 Electromechanical systems
- '70 Stored program control (and CCS)
- '80 SS7 research
- '85 SS7 deployment
- '90 IN and CS releases
- '98 New versions of IN

Figure 1–17 Relative "intelligence" in the network (on a scale of 0 to 10). *(Source:* **Conference on Intelligent Networks, May 9, 1996, London, IBC Technical Services, Ltd.)**

Consequently, the CCITT began work in the mid-1970s on a new generation signaling system. These efforts resulted in the publication of SS7 in 1980 with extensive improvements published in 1984 and again in 1988. Today, SS7 and variations are implemented throughout the world. Indeed, SS7 has found its way into other communications architectures such as personal communications services (PCS) and global systems for mobile communications (GSM) and, of course, the IN.

SS7 greatly improved in "intelligence" in the network, and subsequent efforts built on the SS7 architecture to make the SCP and SSP more intelligent and responsive to the customer's requirements. These efforts found their way into the IN standards that are discussed in later chapters.

Well, on a scale of 1 to 10, does Figure 1–17 imply that we are at the end of IN road? Hardly. The figure depicts the relative "intelligence" of the technologies. The groundwork for IN is just being laid. If we were to examine and redraw this figure a few years from now, it is likely that the out years will build on the 1998 bar. But, the next few years will be ones of incremental progress, not the large changes shown in the figure when stored program control and SS7 came into the industry.

SUMMARY

The intelligent network has gradually evolved since the early 1970s, and its growth accelerated with the advent of 800 services and the deployment of SS7. With the publication and implementation of the ITU-T and Bellcore standards, the stage is set for extensive and international deployment of IN.

2

Key Components of the Intelligent Network

T his chapter describes the key components that operate in the intelligent network. The functions of these components are described, as well as how they are deployed in SS7/IN nodes. The chapter also introduces the ITU-T and Bellcore call models for IN services.

SPECIAL IN COMPONENTS

During the evolution from a conventional service-specific environment to a service-independent environment, it was recognized that the implementation of IN-specific components would enhance and improve the network, mainly by aiding the rapid creation of services and the efficient maintenance of these services. These components are called the *service creation environment (SCE),* the *service management system (SMS),* the *intelligent peripheral (IP),* the *adjunct,* and the *network access point (NAP).* Their position in the IN topology is illustrated in Figure 2–1. Notice that I have included a "cloud" that depicts the SS7 backbone. Inside this cloud are the STPs and their associated links. With a few exceptions (explained shortly), the IN does not impose additional tasks for the STPs.

The SCE provides design and implementation tools to assist in creating and customizing services in the SCP. The SMS is a database man-

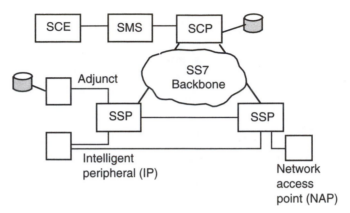

Note: The SCP, adjunct, and intelligent peripheral house the AIN applications programs.
where:
SCE   Service creation environment
SMS   Service management system

Figure 2–1   Special AIN components.

agement system. It is used to manage the master database that controls the IN customer services. This service includes ongoing database maintenance, backup and recovery, log management, and audit trails.

The intelligent peripheral was introduced in Chapter 1. It can connect to an AIN call. It provides the following services: (1) tone generation, (2) voice recognition, (3) playback, (4) compression, (5) call control, (6) record, and (7) DTMF detection and collection. As Figure 2–1 illustrates, the IP is connected to one or more SSPs. It is designed to be application-independent, and to support generic services for more than one application.

The adjunct was also introduced in Chapter 1. It performs the same operations as an SCP, but it is configured for one (or few) services for a single switch. The connection is through a high-speed link in order to support user requests that need a fast response. Other switches that wish to use the services of the adjunct must come through the SSP to which the adjunct is directly connected.

The NAP is a switch that has no IN functions. It is connected off an SSP, and interfaces to trunks with SS7 messages or frequency tones. Based on the called and calling number received at the NAP, it may route the call to its attached SSP or IN services.

The IN STPs perform two functions beyond their usual operations. First, they can employ pseudo-addressing that enables them to balance the load between two or more SCPs (which overrides the MTP 3 routing

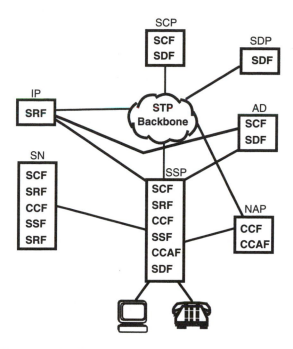

Figure 2–2   IN physical nodes and functional entities.

table entries). Second, they can employ alternate routing in the event of a problem in the network.

THE FUNCTIONAL ENTITIES AND PHYSICAL NODES

Figure 2–2 shows the IN physical nodes and their functional entities.[1] These entities are summarized as follows (also, see Figure 3–5 and Table 3–1 in Chapter 3):

- *Service switching function (SSF):* Provides the means to recognize calls requiring IN service processing and to interact with call pro-

---

[1]The ITU-T specifications Q.1205 is used as the model for this figure with the Q.1215 updates. Be aware that it is a model and in an actual implementation several IN components may operate in one node or may be combined together in a node. For example, a service node can combine the functions of an IP and an SCP, which means that the SCF, SDF, and SRF components are combined into this one node. The idea behind these options is to give vendors and service providers flexibility in implementing the IN technology.

cessing and the service logic on behalf of those calls. When associated with the CCF, it provides the functions needed for interactions between the CCF and the SCF. It is also used to extend the capability of the CCF to recognize IN service control triggers (discussed in Chapter 5). It manages the signaling between the CCF and the SCF, and modifies call processing functions in the CCF (if needed) to handle requests for IN provided service usage under control of the SCF. The SSF is managed by the SMF.

- *Call control function (CCF) (or call processing):* Provides the means for establishing and controlling bearer services on behalf of network users. It supports requests from the CCAF to set up and tear-down connections, and associates the CCAF functional entities to each connection instance. It is also involved in trigger operations (by passing events to the SSF). The CCF is managed by the SMF.

- *Call control agent function (CCAF):* Provides users with access to the services and represents the users to call processing. The CCAF represents the interface between the user and the network control functions. It interacts with the user for all activities pertaining to an IN operation, and accesses the CCF's service-providing capabilities for call or an IN service. It also relays CCF information about the call or service back to the user.

- *Service control function (SCF):* Contains IN service logic providing the logical control to be applied to a call involving an IN service. The SCF handles service-related processing activities such as analysis, translation, screening, and routing. It interacts with other functional entities as needed to obtain information to process a call or IN service. The SCF is managed by the SMF.

- *Service data function (SDF):* Handles service-related and network data. It provides the SCF with a logical view of the data. The SDF contains data that directly relates to the provision or operation of IN services and may include access to user-defined service-related data. The SDF is managed by the SMF.

- *Specialized resource function (SRF):* Provides end-user interaction with the IN through control over resources such as DTMF receivers, voice recognition capabilities, protocol conversion, and announcements. The SRF is managed by the SMF.

- *Service management function (SMF):* Provides the service provisioning, deployment, and management control. The SMF allows access to all IN functional entities for the transfer of information related to service logic and service data.

- *Service management access function (SMAF):* Controls access to service management functions.
- *Service creation environment function (SCEF):* Supports the creation, verification, and testing of new IN services.

The Physical Entities

In addition to the ongoing SS7 functions that the physical entities provide, they also support the IN operations (see Table 2–1). Moreover, additional physical entities are added to the overall system. The service switching point (SSP) continues to provide users the access to the network through the local exchange. The SSP also provides the user with the interface to the IN functions. This component is tasked with detection capabilities, which means that it must detect user requests for IN services. It also interfaces with other physical entities that contain a service control function (SCF). The SSP contains a call control function (CCF) and a service switching function (SSF). And, if it is acting as a local exchange, it also contains a call control agent function (CCAF). As options, it may contain a service control function (SCF), a specialized resource function (SRF), and a service data function (SDF). If network access points (NAPs) are employed, the SSP provides IN services to the users that are connected to NAPs.

The NAP is not a fully functional IN node. It contains only the CCAF and CCF functional entities. It does not communicate with an SCF but is able to determine if IN services are to be invoked to support a user request. If such an event occurs, NAP sends these calls to an SSP.

The service control points (SCPs) are connected to the SSPs by the SS7 network and contains Service Logic Programs (SLPs) and associated data to provide the IN services. The SCP contains a SCF and a SDF. The SCP can access data in a service data point (SDP, discussed next) either directly or through the signaling network. And, the SDP may be in the same or a different network as the SCP. The SCP can also be connected to IPs (also discussed shortly).

The SDP contains the customer data, which is usually accessed during the excution of an IN service. The SDP contains an SDF.

The Intelligent Peripheral (IP) provides a number of services in the IN network such as voice recognitions, announcements, dual-tone multi-frequency (DTMF) digit collection. The IP can connect directly to one-or-more SSPs or may connect through the signaling network. The IP contains the SRF.

The adjunct (AD) is a physical entity that is the equivalent to an SCP and it contains the same functional entities. The difference between the AD and the SCP, is that the AD is connected directly to an SSP through a high-speed interface. The idea of this arrangement is to provide a very fast service for certain features in the IN. The AD can be connected to more than one SSP and an SSP can be connected to multiple ADs.

The service node (SN) is designed to provide interactions with users as well as control IN services. It communicates directly with SSPs and contains an SCF, SDF, SRF, and an SSF/CCF. In the SN, the SSF/CCF is not accessible by external SCFs and is closely coupled to the specific SCF operating within the SN.

The SN operates in a similar fashion to the AD in that the SCF receives messages from the SSP and executes SLPs. The deployment of the SRF in an SN allows the SN to interact with users in a fashion similar to that of the IP.

The service switching and control point (SSCP) is a combined SCP and SSP operating in a single node. It contains an SCF, SDF, CCAF, CCF, and SSF. The deployment of an SSCP is completely dependent upon the specific operator providing IN services.

PLACEMENT OF THE FUNCTIONAL ENTITIES

Table 2–1 is a summary of the functional entities and the placement in the IN physical entities. The first column of the table names the functional entity. The second column provides a brief description of its functions, and the third column shows the placement of the functional entity in an SS7/IN node (the physical entity).

IN Vendors' Platforms

A survey was made of the major AIN platform vendors by the type of equipment they offered and this information is shown in Table 2–2 (*Source:* Profiting from AIN Conference, Radisson Hotel, Atlanta, GA, January 29–30, 1997, Jerome Krasner, Conference Presenter). Be aware that the IN market place is changing and this table should be used to gain a general idea of the marketplace.

THE BELLCORE AND ITU-T SPECIFICATIONS

In March 1993, the ITU-T approved a set of capabilities for intelligent networks called Capability Set 1 (CS-1). This CS is designed to introduce a range of services and support the rapid customizing of the ser-

Table 2–1   Functional Entities and Their Placements

Functional Entity	Description	Placement
Call control access function (CAF)	Allows user to access the CCF; handles call setup, termination, hold-on, etc., can also provide user with CLASS (Customer Local Area Signaling Services).	SSP, NAP
Call control function (CCF)	Supports establishment of conventional bearer services.	SSP
Service switching function (SSF)	Recognizes calls requiring IN service processing. Interacts with call processing and service logic.	SSP
Service control function (SCF)	Furnishes control for a call requiring IN service and handles service-related processing activities.	SCP, AD, SN
Service data function (SDF)	Supports access to network data and provides a logical view of the data to the SCF.	SCP, AD, SN
Specialized resource function (SRF)	Supports user interaction with the IN resources through interaction with resources such as DTMF, voice recognition, announcements.	SN, IP
Service management function (SMF)	Allows access to IN resources for the transfer of information.	SMS
Service creation environment function (SCEF)	Deals with the creation, validation, and evaluation of new IN services	SCE

where:
    IP   = Intelligent peripheral
    NAP = Network access point
    SCE = Service creation environment
    SCP = Service control point
    SMS = Service management system
    SN   = Service node
    SSP = Service switching point
Source: Conference on Intelligent Networks, May 9, 1996, sponsored by IBC Technical Services Ltd.

vice implementations. The ITU-T CS has the status of an international standard, due to the position of ITU-T in the standards organizations' ladder.

In North America, the tendency is not to follow the formal international standards, and Bellcore has published a set of specifications known as the Advanced Intelligent Network (AIN) Release 0.1, 0.2, and 0.X. The concepts behind Bellcore's AIN specifications are in accord with the ITU-T IN. The view of Bellcore is that its approach is "more implementable and deployable."

In 1996, Bellcore released yet another version of its AIN specification, which is intended to supplant AIN 0.1 and AIN 0.2. This revision is

Table 2–2   Vendors' Offerings in the Platforms

IN Platform Vendors	SCP	IP	Associated SCEs
AccessLine Technologies		x	x
AG Communications Systems		x	x
Bellcore	x	x	x
Boston Technology		x	x
Brite Voice Systems		x	x
Centigram Communications	x	x	
Cognitronics		x	x
DGM&S	x	x	x
Digital Equipment	x	x	x
Digital Sound		x	x
DSC Communications	x	x	x
Ericsson	x	x	x
Glenayre		x	x
GNP Computers		x	x
Hewlett-Packard	x	x	x
IBM	x	x	x
Integrated Micro Products	x		x
InterVoice		x	x
Lucent Technologies	x	x	x
Motorola	x	x	x
Newbridge Networks	x	x	x
NewNet	x	x	
Nokia Telecommunications	x	x	x
Nortel	x	x	x
Octel Communications		x	
Open Development	x		
Precision Systems		x	
Sequent Computer Systems	x	x	
Siemens	x	x	x
Stratus Computers	x		x
Sun Microsystems	x	x	
Tandem Telecom	x	x	x
Texas Instruments		x	x
Texas Microsystems	x	x	
Unisys		x	
Voicetek		x	x

published in Bellcore GR-1298-CORE, Issue 3, July 1996, Revision 1, November 1996.

Once again in Europe, the European Telecommunications Standards Institute (ETSI) Core INAP (Intelligent Network Application Protocol) activity is another part of IN. This effort was initiated by operators and equipment manufacturers. According to IN/AIN designers, using the similar call model specified in CS-1, this activity concentrates on the definition of procedures among the SSP, SCP, and IP. ETSI Core INAP activities target improving the content of ITU's interface recommendation for IN CS-1 by defining a more detailed version of the interface for the ETSI standards, then reworking the results as contributions into ITU's IN CS-1R.

Thus far, these efforts are reflected in several ITU-T and Bellcore specifications, which are listed in Tables 2–3, 2–4, and 2–5.

The ITU-T IN Recommendations are published as the Q.12xy Series, where y reflects the topic of the Recommendation, and x indicates if the topic is general (x = 0), pertaining to Capability Set 1 (CS-1) (x = 1), or pertaining to Capability Set 2 (CS-2) (x = 2). Table 2–5 lists the ITU-T IN recommendations for CS-1. The CS-2 recommendations use the same numbering scheme as the entries in the table, with the third digit changed for the following CS-2 documents: Q.1220, Q.1221, Q.1222, Q.1223, Q.1224, Q.1225, Q.1228, and Q.1229.

The CS-1 refinements activity provided significant detail for multi-vendor capability and convergence between ITU CS and AIN streams.

Table 2–3   Bellcore AIN Documents

Release	Document #	Document Title
AIN 0.1	TR-NWT-001284	AIN 0.2 Switching System Generic Requirements
AIN 0.1	TR-NWT-001285	AIN 0.1 Switching System-Service Control Point Application Protocol interface Generic Requirements
AIN 0.2	GR-1298-CORE	AIN 0.2 SSP Requirements, Issue 1
AIN 0.2	GR-1299-CORE	AIN 0.2 SSP-SCP/Adjunct Application Protocol Interface Generic Requirements, Issue 1
AIN 0.2	GR-1229-CORE	AIN 0.2 SSP-IP Interface Generic Requirements, Issue 1
AIN 1	GR-1280-CORE	AIN SCP Generic Requirements
AIN 1	GR-1286-CORE	AIN OS-SCP Interface Generic Requirement, Issue 1
AIN 1	GR-1299-CORE	AIN 0.1 SSP-SCP/Adjunct Application Protocol Interface Generic Requirements, Issue 2
AIN 1	GR-1298-CORE	AIN Generic Requirements, Issue 3

Table 2–4   INA Specifications

Document #	Document Title
SR-NWT-002280	An Introduction to the INA Field Experiment Initiative, Issue 1
SR-NWT-002281	INA Cycle 1 Documentation Road Map, Issue 2
SR-NWT-002282	INA Cycle 1 Framework Architecture, Issue 2
SR-TSV-002283	INA Cycle 1 Contract Specification, Issue 2
SR-NWT-002284	INA Cycle 1 Distributed Processing Environment Specification, Issue 2
SR-TSV-002285	INA Cycle 1 Trading and Naming Specification, Issue 2
SR-NWT-002286	INA Cycle 1 Network Management Functional Architecture, Issue 2
SR-NWT-002287	INA Cycle 1 Management Information Model, Issue 2
SR-NWT-002288	INA Cycle 1 Service Management Architecture, Issue 2
SR-NWT-002289	INA Cycle 1 Protocol Specification, Issue 1
SR-TSV-002290	INA Cycle 1 Security Specification, Issue 1
SR-TSV-002291	INA Cycle 1 Data Management Specification, Issue 1
SR-TSV-002660	INA Cycle 1 Communications Management Architecture, Issue 2
SR-NWT-002804	INA Cycle 1 Contracts and DPE Experiments Report, Issue 1
SR-NWT-002806	INA Cycle 1 Configuration Experiments Report, Issue 1

Network providers still need to specify detail with the vendors for market-specific requirements. AIN Rel 0.1/0.2 provides this detail for the North American market, including specific interworking for UNI and NNI (as examples, DS1 and ISUP) North American protocol variants.

ETSI network operators have agreed on a common subset of functionality and further details are needed for specific interworkings and network operator options. CS-2 scope provides a significant challenge to specify adequate details for multivendor compatibility.

Rel 0.1 handles the basic call processing for a two-party call. It is routing-oriented and has translation and number substitution capabilities. It supports an IP that is internally integrated to an SSP. Besides the switch-based call processing, a Rel 0.1 SSP can perform the following functions: triggering, querying, response processing, trigger activation/deactivation, termination notification, call interaction, monitor resource, and code gapping.

Rel 0.2 is built on Rel 0.1. It offers an incremental SSP and protocol message set. The SSP and SSP-SCP interface functionality is backward compatible with that defined for Rel 0.1. Rel 0.2 functionality is significantly extended compared to Rel 0.1. The extended capabilities include more terminating triggers, triggers for busy and no answer state, and interactions with a special resource IP. Above Rel 0.1, Rel 0.2 SSP can per-

Table 2–5   ITU-T IN Recommendations

Recommendation #	Title
Q.1200	General Series Intelligent Network Recommendation Structure
Q.1201	Principles of Intelligent Network Architecture
Q.1202	Intelligent Network-Service Plane Architecture
Q.1203	Intelligent Network-Global Functional Plane
Q.1204	Intelligent Network-Distributed Functional Plane
Q.1205	Intelligent Network-Physical Plane
Q.1208	General Aspects of the Intelligent Network Application Protocol (INAP)
Q.1210	Q-Series Intelligent Network Recommendation Structure
Q.1211	Introduction to Intelligent Network Capability Set 1
Q.1213	Intelligent Network-Global Functional Plane for CS-1
Q.1214	Intelligent Network-Distributed Functional Plane for CS-1
Q.1215	Intelligent Network-Physical Plane for CS-1
Q.1218	Interface Recommendation for CS-1
Q.1219	Intelligent Network User's Guide for CS-1
Q.1290	Glossary of Terms Used in the Definition of Intelligent Network Applications

Note: CS-2 Recommendations use the same numbering scheme as above, with third digit changed for the following CS-2 documents: Q.1220, Q.1221, Q.1222, Q.1223, Q.1224, Q.1225, Q.1228, Q.1229.

form these additional functions: next event list and event detection, IP interface, procedures for bridging a receiver and an I to a customer, ISDN/AIN interworking, feature interaction, fault handling, and automatic message accounting.

CS-1 provides a broader view of IN and a larger IN functionality converge compared to Rel 0.1 and Rel 0.2. CS-1 addresses issues beyond the functional/physical plane of the network. In addition to the network entities, SCP/SSP interface and IP interface, CS-1 also defines the SSP/service node interface, as well as SCP/SDP interface, and direct SCP/IP interface (none of these are included in Rel 0.1/0.2).

ETSI INAP defines the Intelligent Network Application Protocol (INAP) required for the support of CS-1. It is intended for the development of INAP in the existing ISDN and PSTN. ETSI INAP concentrates on the definition of a more detailed and deployable version of the interfaces and procedures between SSP/IP and the SCP as defined by CS-1. It uses the same call model specified in CS-1, but some operations in CS-1 are not covered in ETSI INAP.

SUMMARY

The key components of the IN were explained in this chapter. It is evident that the IN components and their functional entities are integrated into the SS7 topology. Of course, the ITU-T and Bellcore call models are critical components in the IN. Their documents were listed and summarized as a prelude to more detailed explanations in subsequent chapters.

3

The IN Model

This chapter introduces the IN Call Model, as published by the ITU-T, which is also known as the IN conceptual model (INCM). The INCM capability sets (CS) introduced in Chapter 2 are explained in more detail. The four planes of the INCM are analyzed, with emphasis on the important role that service independent building blocks (SIBs) play in the model. The IN functional entities are revisited, and the placement in SS7 nodes is explained in more detail.

THE ITU MODEL

Intelligent networks are modeled through the IN conceptual model (INCM). This model is published in ITU-T Recommendation Q.1201, with supplementary information in Q.1203, Q.1204, and Q.1213. It is used as a tool in the development of what are called *IN capability sets (CS)*.

The model is organized around three principal elements: (a) basic call processing, (b) "hooks", and (c) IN service logic.

Basic call processing (BCP) is the conventional operation of setting up and disconnecting a call and does not entail special features. BCP must be: (a) service-independent, (b) organized into modular subprocesses, and (c) exhibit the characteristics of atomic actions.[1] These requirements are facilitated with the use of software/data basetools such as object-oriented languages and systems (for example, see the next chapter for a discussion on one such tool called CORBA)

"Hooks" form the interface between BCP modules and the IN service modules. They are capable of (a) suspending the BCP operations, (b) starting the IN operations, (c) completing the IN operations, and (d) resuming the execution of the BCP. In practice, they are implemented as an application programming interface (API), with software function/library calls.

IN service logic consists of the software to provide the IN supplementary services, which interact with BCP through the hooks. Once involved, the IN service logic controls the manner in which interaction occurs between BCP and the IN modules.

As Figure 3–1 shows, INCM consists of four planes. Each of these planes provides an abstract view of the IN capabilities. The concept is based (usually) on taking a top-down view in regard to services and a bottom-up view with respect to the bearer capabilities (the underlying network capabilities). Of course, like all models, the INCM is a tool that is useful in an abstract manner to describe the characteristics and capabilities of an IN. Certainly, this model does not reflect an actual IN. Like all the models in the standards groups, it is used as a conceptual reference guide for designers. But, unlike some models published by the standards organizations, the INCM is a useful, pragmatic tool for the IN designer.

The top plane in the model is called the service plane. It is so named because it provides a service-oriented view (the user's view) of the IN capabilities. Each service in the service plane is grouped into units with each service designated as a service feature (SF). An example of a service feature is user authentication; another is call queuing. A service feature is (ideally) service independent. To illustrate, the service feature user authentication is applicable to most any type of call. Likewise, call queuing may be used in 800 and 911 services.

From these two examples, we can see how the SF aspect of the model provides a pragmatic common-sense framework for an intelligent network. In so many words, why reinvent the wheel? Since many ser-

---

[1]A subprocess is atomic if, say subprocess X, is not aware of the existence of other active subprocesses and other subprocesses are not aware of subprocess X, during the time that process X is executing. The subprocess performing an action does not communicate with other subprocesses while the action is being performed. The subprocess performing the action can detect no changes except those performed by itself and it does not reveal its state changes until the action is complete.

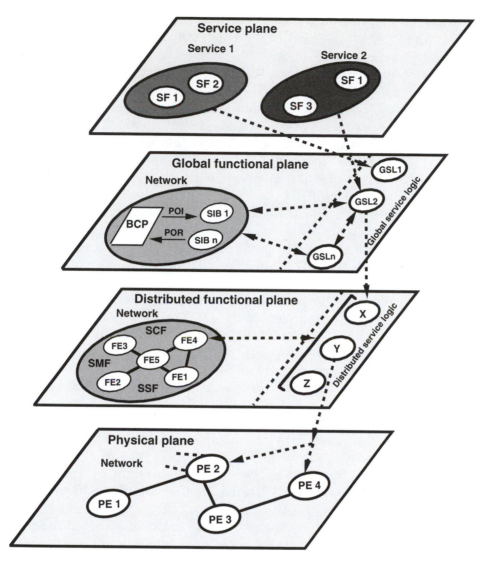

Figure 3–1 IN conceptual model (INCM).

vices need common software modules, the IN model identifies these modules, and (as demonstrated later) provides guidance on how they are designed, coded, and executed. This approach provides a "plug and play" aspect to the service features.

Each service feature is a description of a single set of global service logic (GSL). By a set, I mean that a service feature can be assembled from components such as software routines. Indeed, GSL is program code.

With the high-level service plane view, there is no correlation of the service and the physical network on which it is deployed nor the specific SF on that physical network.

The global functional plane (GFP) is the next plane in the model. This plane deals with service independent building blocks (SIBs). In turn, the GSL, described earlier, defines how the SIBs are combined to provide service features. It also describes the interactions between a dedicated SIB, which is known as a basic call process (BCP). This special SIB interacts with the other SIBs. To iterate, a set of global service logic defines (in the terms of SIBs) a service feature. Therefore, the GSL defines where and how the SIBs can interact with the BCP. SIBs are service independent, reusable across service features, and available on a network-wide basis.

The GFP also describes the point of initiation (POI), and the point of return (POR) between the BCP and one SIB or a sequence of SIBs, executed as a chain.

The next plane in the model is the distributed functional plane. This plane provides a distributed view of the IN. The view is in terms of a set of functional entities (FEs), which define network functionality. Each of these FEs is able to perform specific actions and is a computational object. The FEs can perform functional entity actions (FEAs). Indeed, one way to view the functional entity is that it is actually comprised of FEAs. In turn, FEAs are comprised of elementary functions (EFs). The best way to think of the EFs is that they are the atomic units of the FEAs. However, the EF is mentioned only in a general way in the standards and is left for further study.

Another way to view the FEAs is that their chaining and sequence within the FE make up the SIB. Stated another way, an SIB is instantiated by the FEs and their FEAs.

Yet another way to view the operations in the distributed functional plane is that an SIB in the global functional plane is broken down into the distributed functional plane into sets of client/server systems. Consequently, as we said before, each FE is defined to perform the FEAs. SIBs are actually implemented by a sequence of FEAs performed (as we said earlier) by specific FEs.

The actual protocols in the INAP occur when SIBs need to send information between FEs, which in essence allows the SIB to be realized. The information flows then provide the protocol in the physical plane.

Finally, the physical plane models the different entities and protocols that exist within the intelligent network. This plane defines physical entities (PEs) and the interfaces between the PEs. It defines where the FEs emanating from the distributed functional plane are located. The abstract view of the planes is decompressed to a less abstract view at the physical plane. For example, PEs within this plane could be SS7 switching points or control points.

One way to view this model is to think of the upper two planes concentrating on how services are created, with the ability to create building blocks for these services. In contrast, the lower two levels, especially the physical plane, are concerned with specific networks and service provisioning.

RELATIONSHIPS BETWEEN THE PLANES

As depicted by the arrows in Figure 3–1, the service features in the service plane are realized in the global functional plane with a GSL and SIBs (including BCP).

The SIBs in the global functional plane are present in the FEs in the distributed functional plane, and a SIB may be instantiated in more than one FE. Each set of GSL in the global functional plane is realized by one or more DSLs in the distributed functional plane.

The FEs in the distributed functional plane are mapped to the PEs in the physical plane. Each FE is mapped into one PE.

THE SIBs

The ITU-T Q.1203 and Q.1213 contains information on the CS-1 SIBs and Q.1214 defines how 14 SIBs (the basic call process is the fifteenth) are to operate. The following SIBs are defined in these standards.

Algorithm SIB: This SIB performs a computation on the data. Initially, it was designed as a complex set of computations, but it was narrowed to perform simple incrementing/decrementing of a call specific variable by a verified integer number.

Authenticate SIB: This SIB provides authentication support. It can be implemented to (1) check only a user name and password, (2) execute a more complex authentication operation such as encryption, or (3) provide no authentication.

Charge SIB: This SIB defines how a call is to be charged. It supports operations such as split charging or reverse charging. It also identifies the resources that are to be charged such as circuits and messages.

Compare SIB: This SIB compares an identifier (any type of variable) with a reference value. The results are (1) greater than, (2) less than, or (3) equal to.

Distribution SIB: The distribution SIB is similar to the compare SIB but it is more powerful. It supports the distribution of calls to other ends. One example is the distribution of calls on a percentage basis where one operator (agent) gets more calls than the other.

Limit SIB: This SIB limits the number of calls that are processed in the AIN. This operation may seem contradictory but it is used to proactively manage potential congestion rather than merely responding to it.

Log call information SIB: This SIB logs information about calls such as call attempts, disconnect times, and dialed numbers.

Queue SIB: This SIB queues incoming calls when agents are busy. Typically, the customer receives an announcement asking it to wait. The queue SIB also provides an option to redirect or suspend the call.

Screen SIB: This SIB compares a value (for examples, a PIN, originating number, or terminating number) to a list of stored values called a screen list. It has filtering capabilities that, for example, can allow or disallow the completion of a call.

Service data management SIB: This SIB modifies, stores, corrects, and retrieves information about a customer. In essence, it has a database management capability.

Status notification SIB: This SIB is used to monitor network resources to determine their states or status (for example, are lines/trunks up, down, idle, or busy?).

Translate SIB: This SIB receives input information and translates this information to different output information.

User-interaction SIB: This SIB is used to exchange information between a called or calling party and the IN.

Verify SIB: This SIB is an editor that checks for the syntax of the information as being correct or incorrect.

Basic call process SIB: This SIB is responsible for basic call processing.

THE SERVICE PLANE

Figure 3–2 provides more information on the service plane and a list that summarizes key points about the service plane. This plane describes and stocks the services that are supported by an IN. The first step in building an intelligent network is to identify and explain a set of services for the customer. The next step is to identify the features for the services and then (as we will describe later in more detail) identify (select, add, modify) a set of SIBs to support the service.

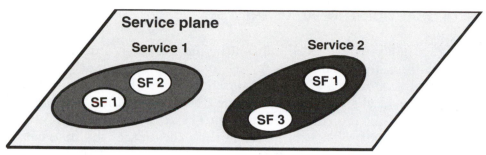

Key Points:
- The term "IN service" is misleading: IN is service independent.
- IN standardizes the procedures and protocols to bring in IN services to a network.
- IN service plane describes and stocks the services that are support by an IN.
- A service may be contradictory to another service.
- Each service becomes a specific commercial service.
- A service feature (SF) can be used with more than one service.
- A service may be customized.
- Services (and service features) must be single-ended.
- A service feature must have only one point of control.

Figure 3–2   The service plane in more detail.

Several aspects of this process warrant comment. First, a service may be contradictory to another service. For example, a call originating in the United States with call forwarding service may be contradictory to call restriction, if a customer is not allowed to make calls to a foreign country.

Second, a service feature (SF) can be used with more than one service. Indeed, reusability is important in order to capitalize on the code that can be applied to more than one service.

Third, it is obviously intended that each service becomes a specific commercial service. After all, why spend resources on developing a service if it does not produce revenue?

Fourth, services (and service features) must be single-ended. This term means that a service feature that is invoked to support a party participating in a call is independent of any other party that is involved in the call. The same service feature can be used by another party, but the instances of these service features must not interact with each other (once again, adhering to the atomic action concept).

Finally, a service feature must have only one point of control. Controlled by only one service control function (SCF). This rule keeps the different processes tightly coupled to one machine and not coupled at all to processes in other machines.

THE GLOBAL FUNCTIONAL PLANE

Figure 3–3 provides more information on the global functional plane and a list that summarizes key points about the functional plane. It is composed of programs and instructions that are called service independent building blocks (SIBs). This plane also defines the global service logic (GSL) and the interfaces between the GSL and the basic call process (BCP). The GSL stipulates the order of the execution of the instructions in the IN; that is to say, the order of the invocation of the SIBs.

This figure also shows the point-of-initiation (POI) and the point-of-return (POR). The POI is the interface between the BCP and the GSL and defines the point where the BCP operations are suspended. In turn, the POR defines the point where the suspended operations are resumed. We shall see later that this interface is modeled on a remote procedure call (RPC) architecture.

THE DISTRIBUTED FUNCTIONAL PLANE

Figure 3–4 provides more information on the distributed functional plane and a list that summarizes key points about the distributed functional plane. The distributed functional plane consists of a set of objects

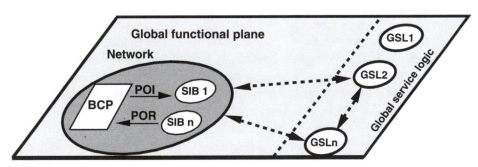

Key Points:
- Service composed of programs and instructions is defined in this plane.
- Instructions are called service independent building blocks (SIBs).
- Defines interfaces between basic call process (BCP) and global service logic (GSL).
- GSL stipulate the order of instructions (the SIBs).
- Interface of BCP and GSL SIBs is through point of initiation (POI) and point of return (POR).
- Interface is modeled on a remote procedure call (RPC) architecture.

Figure 3–3   The global functional plane in more detail.

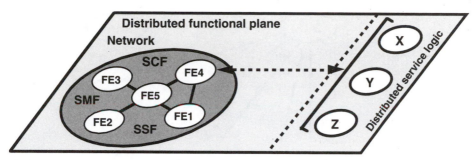

Key Points:
- Network is viewed as a set of objects called functional entities (FEs).
- FEs exchange information with each other with information flows (IFs).
- IFs can be remote procedure calls (RPCs), function calls, or electronic/fiber signals.
- FEs are abstract models of software and hardware used in the network elements.
- FEs are grouped together as: (a) FEs that execute services and (b) FEs that create and manage services.
- The basic call state model (BCSM) is introduced as part of this plane (and in the ITU-T standards).

Figure 3–4   The distributed functional plane in more detail.

called *functional entities (FEs)*. The FEs exchange information with each other with information flows (IFs). The IFs can take the form of remote procedure calls, program function calls, or physical signals.

FUNCTIONAL ENTITIES

As stated earlier, the intelligent network architecture is based on functional entities (see Figure 3–5). These entities, introduced in Chapter 2, pertain to service control, switching, service management, and triggering of events in the intelligent network. These functional entities are organized into three broad categories: basic call handling functions, service execution functions, and service management functions. Figure 3–5 also shows the type of traffic flow between the functional entities: (a) not standardized, (b) bearer connection control relationship (BCP-type operations), (c) non-IN call control, and (d) IN call control.

The basic call handling functions are divided into the call control agent function (CCAF) and the connection control function (CCF). These entities represent specific elements within a network, such as the telephone network or an ISDN. The CCAF is the interface into the user device. In turn, the CCAF interfaces into the CCF. The CCF is responsible for basic call processing operations.

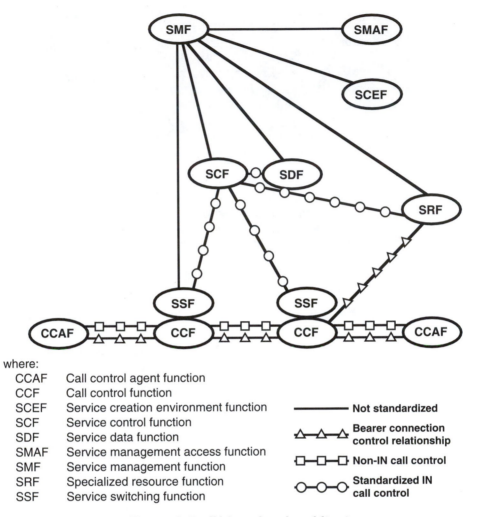

Figure 3–5   IN functional architecture.

The service execution functions are organized around (1) the service switching function (SSF), (2) the service control function (SCF), (3) the service data function (SDF), and (4) the specialized resource function (SRF). These functions are responsible for the supplementary services in the intelligent network. The SSF provides switching functions to the SCF. In turn, the SCF controls resources at the switch or, alternately, an intelligent peripheral (discussed later).

The service data function is also known as the specialized data function. As the name implies, it supports the service data (which includes customer data and internal network data). It allows the SCF to access this data whenever necessary.

The last function in the service execution functions is the specialized resource function (SRF). It provides additional support operations for managing intelligent peripherals. Examples of its operations are the management of tape recordings for playing announcements and overall information collection and analysis functions.

The system management function (SMF) is made up of the service management access function (SMAF) and the service creation environment function (SCE). The overall operations of SMF include the introduction and provisioning of services, as well as their maintenance. The SMF interfaces with the SMAF, which is responsible for providing a MAN-machine interface to this SMF. The last function in this model is the SCEF, which is used for the testing of the specifications of the IN services.

THE PHYSICAL PLANE

Figure 3–6 provides more information on the physical plane and a list that summarizes key points about it. The physical plane describes the placement of the FEs in the physical equipment in the network. It describes the interfaces among the FEs in relation to the physical components in the network such as the service switching point (SSP), service control point (SCP), and so on.

IN FUNCTIONS AND SS7 NODES

ITU-T Recommendation Q.1211 defines how the distributed functional plane allows the FEAs to be grouped into functional areas, as shown in Figure 3–7. For example, areas such as service control functions and switching functions communicate through the use of actual protocol flows across reference points, labeled A, B, C, D, E, and F and shown in this figure.

As we shall see later, this information flow is based on message protocols and defined by the presentation layer's Abstract Syntax Notation 1 (ASN.1). The other interfaces shown in Figure 3–7 have not yet been standardized by the standards bodies.

Table 3–1 shows the relationships of the IN functional entities to the physical entities, which are the physical components in the network.

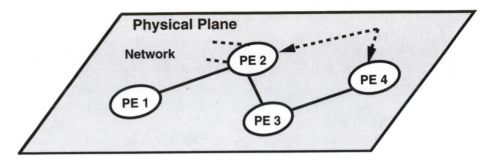

Key Points:
- Describes the placement of the FEs in the physical components in the network
- Describes the interfaces among the FEs:
  Service switching point (SSP)
  Service control point (SCP)
  Service data point (SDP)
  Intelligent peripheral (IP)
  Adjunct (AD)
  Service node (SN)
  Service management point (SMP)
  Service management agent point (SMAP)
  Service creation environment point (SCEP)
- Describes IN in relation to layer 7 of the OSI Model, including the application process (AP), and the application entity (AE)

Figure 3–6   The physical plane in more detail.

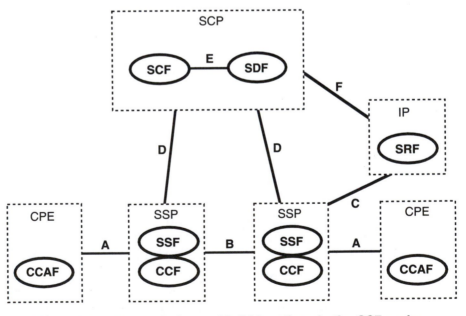

Figure 3–7   Physical plane with IN functions in the SS7 nodes.

Table 3–1   The Relationships of the Functional Entities to the Physical Entities

	SSF/CCF	SCF	SDF	SRF	SMF	SCEF	SMAF
SSP	M	O	O	O	NA	NA	NA
SCP	NA	M	O	NA	NA	NA	NA
SPD	NA	NA	M	NA	NA	NA	NA
IP	O	NA	NA	M	NA	NA	NA
Adjunct	NA	M	M	NA	NA	NA	NA
Service node	M	M	M	M	NA	NA	NA
SSCP	M	M	M	O	NA	NA	NA
SMP	NA	NA	NA	NA	M	O	O
SCEP	NA	NA	NA	NA	NA	M	NA
SMAP	NA	NA	NA	NA	NA	NA	M

where:

M   = Mandatory
O   = Optional
NA = Not Allowed

EXAMPLE OF THE IN MODEL IN ACTION

An example of the operations of the IN model is provided in Figure 3–8. Note that not all the functional entities in the mode are invoked in this example. This example reflects the "first release" of the ITU-T IN model.

We learned earlier that the CCAF is the interface to the customer. In this example, the CCAF receives a call connection request from the

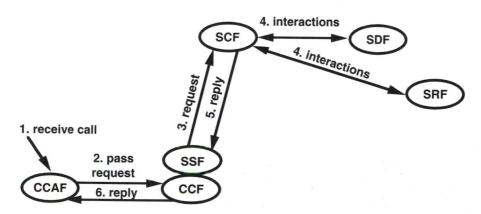

Figure 3–8   An example of the model in operation (one of several scenarios).

user, receives the called party number, and passes this information to the CCF/SSF. In turn, these entities examine the information to determine if they are to process the call as a basic call processing operation or if the information is to be treated as an IN service request. For the latter operation, the request is passed to an appropriate SCF. The SCF then processes the information with the proper IN program and communicates with an SDF and perhaps an SRF to fulfill the request. It then passes the requested information back to the requesting CCF/SSF.

EXAMPLE OF ELEMENT MAPPING

Figure 3–9 is yet another way to view the IN model. It shows the element mapping down through the planes. This view is one of British Telecom's (BT) methods of correlating several of the components in the model.

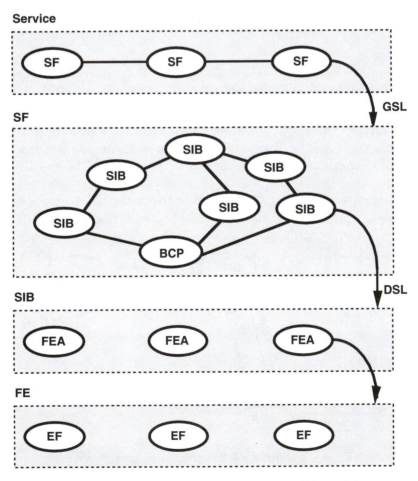

Figure 3–9 Element mapping in the IN model.

This figure should be studied along with Figure 3–1. The only part of this figure that has not been discussed earlier in this chapter is the elementary function (EF). Recall that a functional entity (FE) can perform a variety of functional entity actions (FEAs). Within each FE, multiple FEAs can exist, and may be performed by one or more EFs. So, Figure 3–9 shows the mapping of IN entities from the service plane to the distributed functional plane and the associated decomposition to the EFs.

IN AND THE OSI MODEL

The IN is organized around the OSI Model and uses the OSI concept of application service elements (ASEs) (see Figure 3–10). ASEs represent

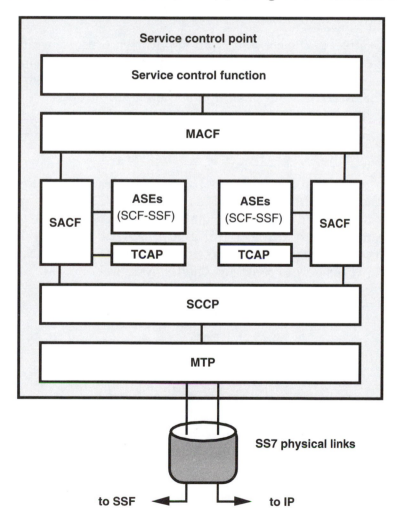

Figure 3–10 The model in a service control point (SCP).

the protocols that operate between peer entities (applications) in the layers. When an application process is running, it is called an application process invocation (API). Each application process invocation can contain one or more application entity invocations (AEIs).

Application associations represent the relationships between the applications. A single association object (SAO) exists for each application within the application entity (AE). This association represents all the capabilities needed for the application association. Other literature refers to the SAO as an application context.

Within the SAO, the ASEs are controlled by a single association control function (SACF). This SACF is responsible for the coordination of the ASEs. In cases where multiple SAOs exist within an application entity, the multiple association control function (MACF) is implemented to govern these multiple SAOs.

Let us return to the concept of an application context, which defines the specific ASEs needed for a particular application association. It is the application context that is negotiated between peer application entities as part of the establishment of an application association.

SUMMARY

The International Standard for IN is set forth in ITU-T Recommendation Q.1201, the IN Conceptual Model (INCM). The INCM consists of four planes and is used to develop capability sets (CSs). While the INCM is indeed a model, it is also a useful and pragmatic tool for the IN software developer, because it provides (with the other IN specifications) detailed guidance for how to construct the IN system.

4

Object-Oriented Finite State Machine Modeling, CORBA, and TMN

T his chapter explains how intelligent networks use object-oriented finite state machine modeling and how the Common Object Request Broker Architecture (CORBA) is used to define how objects interact in a distributed environment. It also explains how CORBA removes an application from concern about the computing platform on which an object operates—obviously an important ingredient in IN. The chapter also introduces the Telecommunications Management Network (TMN) and explains the role of TMN in intelligent networks.

IN AND OTHER TECHNOLOGIES

I have emphasized thus far that the IN concepts have evolved to satisfy more demanding and sophisticated requirements of the user. In parallel with these increased needs for better ways to use the telephone have been technology advances to support these needs. Fast processors, high bandwidth circuits, and object-oriented programming have all contributed to the advancements made in IN.

What is next? Is the implementation of IN the answer to the customer's ultimate needs? The operators, manufacturers, and standards groups are addressing the "What is next?" question in defining what is known as TINA (Telecommunications Information Network Architecture). The idea of TINA is to integrate the TMN, UMTS (Universal Mobile Telecommunications System), ODP (Open Distributed Platform), and the CORBA systems into a unified architecture to support the IN.

TINA is a proposed architecture for intelligent, software/object-oriented platforms. It is an amalgamation of the systems cited in the previous paragraph, and includes additional requirements for the interactions among the hardware and software components that make up TINA.

My initial exposure to TINA left me with the thought, Where does the software trail end from the standpoint of writing code? That is, what is the next standard (software appendage) that one has to add to inculcate all these specifications into a commercial product? And how do all of these systems (with differing software modules) converge?

These questions are the subject of deliberations that are underway in the industry. They are far from resolved, but efforts are being undertaken to answer them. Our task for this chapter is to analyze these systems in the context of their relationship to IN. The focus is on CORBA and TMN; the other systems are discussed later in the book.

OBJECT-ORIENTED FINITE STATE MODELING

The ITU-T IN call model and the Bellcore AIN call model employ finite state machines. This concept describes (models) a system with a boundary on a finite set of states in which the system can operate as well as a finite state of transitions that are possible from one state to another. The approach defines specific inputs to a state and from a state, the concept referred to as "atomic actions" in Chapter 3 (also see Appendix A, Table A–1). Events are associated with the transition from one state to another. For a given event and the parameters associated with that event, the transition from one state to another will always be the same. This means the finite state machine model is deterministic.

The advantage to using finite state machine modeling (FSMM) is that it imposes an unambiguous and strict set of rules on the behavior of the software, if the input to the software is known.

Object-oriented techniques are a valuable tool to describe a system and characterize the states of that system. The system is characterized by objects and these objects represent properties of the system. Each object is described by its unique characteristics (which are called attributes) as well as the actions permitted to manipulate the objects (which are called functions).

In consonance with the design philosophy of an intelligent network and to meet the goals of atomic actions which are fundamental to the intelligent network; the objects must be self-contained, modular processes that can be easily combined to form IN operations. And, of course, they must be generic enough to be reusable, yet lend themselves to be tailored, given their specific inputs.

For intelligent networks, object-oriented FSM provides a valuable tool to describe the system in a relatively simple way: that of modular objects. It supports a vendor-independent tool to describe the IN functions. For the intelligent network, it provides (a) a view of an SSF to an SCF, (b) a means to define the information flows between the SSF and the SCF, and (c) verification of the correct sequencing of functions within an SSF.

In later chapters, more information is provided on the intelligent network finite state machines, the remainder of this chapter will focus on other models and tools to help implement an object-oriented environment for the intelligent network.

CORBA

Concepts

The Common Object Request Broker Architecture (CORBA) is a standardized procedure for defining how objects interact in a distributed environment, based on a client-server model. It is supported by the Object Management Group (OMG), founded in 1989 by several vendors to establish a standardized framework for using object-oriented technology in a distributed network. Four of the principal founders are DEC, Hewlett-Packard, IBM, and Sun.

The basic idea behind CORBA is called *distributed object computing (DOC)*. The idea is to remove an application from concern about the (1) language, (2) hardware, and (3) operating system platforms on which an object operates. So, a client issues a request for a service without concern about these dependencies.

These capabilities are coordinated by the object request broker (ORB) (see Figure 4–1). It acts as a go-between for the client and the server object. In effect, it analyzes the request from the client and chooses the appropriate server object to handle that request. Therefore, it provides the most efficient means for the communications process between the client and the server, and that is why it is called a broker.

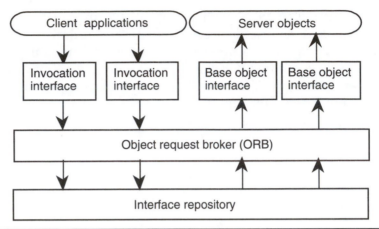

Clients:	Make requests for services from objects
Interface repository:	Database of definitions needed for application
Object request broker (ORB):	Defines how object interacts and communicates (acts as a switch)
Server objects:	Satisfies client request
Interfaces:	Uses a definition language to tie application to objects

Figure 4–1   CORBA architecture.

The interfaces used by the client are independent of the object's implementation, but they are defined in order to provide a standardized environment. The invocation interfaces are used to invoke an operation, and the basic object interfaces provide a specific object implementation to/from the ORB and the object server.

Interfaces

CORBA supports two type of interfaces between the client and ORB (see Figure 4–2). These interfaces are executed with the interface definition language (IDL), a compiler-independent programming language. It is used to specify the client application interface to objects. IDL resembles C++ and includes inheritance features. The IDL is used to code a static invocation interface (SII) or a dynamic invocation interface (DII).

The static invocation interface is nothing more than a simple C call to a completely compiled module. The dynamic invocation interface (DII) is a C call with additional code. It is used when all information is not available at compile time and entails the client application creating a request object that defines the additional information.

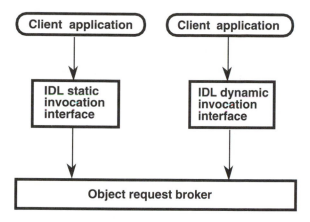

Figure 4–2   Invocation interfaces.

These calls are made with either a synchronous or deferred synchronous request. With the former, the application cannot execute until the server returns the result of request. With the latter, the application can do other work while the request is being processed.

Organization

The object request broker is used through several interfaces. Figure 4–3 shows the relationship of these interfaces with the client and the object implementation. Typically, the client uses the dynamic invocation interface to request a service through the ORB core. The purpose of the dynamic invocation interface is to allow the client to be independent of the interface of the target object, or independent of a dynamic invocation stub. This type of stub is specific to the target object.

The request (up to the object implementation) goes through the IDL skeletons. These are so named because they are specific to an interface and an object adapter. The object adapter's purpose is to allow specific services to be implemented based on the object implementation requirements.

Figure 4–3 also shows the relationships of the stubs and skeletons to the client and the object implementation. The interface repository and implementation repository is made available to the clients and object implementations and/or implemented based on the specific needs of the operation. The implementation repository is set up during the installation and is used during the request delivery to the object implementation.

The ORB can be made up of: (1) operations that are the same for all ORB implementations, (2) operations that are specific to types of objects, or (3) operations that are specific to particular styles of object implementations.

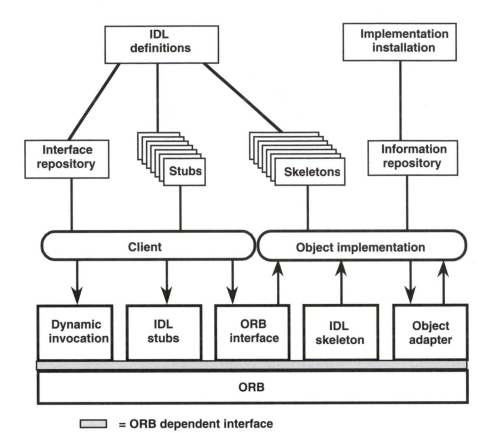

Figure 4–3 CORBA organization.

The ORB interfaces are highlighted in the top part of Figure 4–4. These interfaces define each option for calling the ORB or receiving a call. The dynamic invocation is independent of a target object interface and can be invoked in a somewhat ad hoc fashion. The IDL stub is a specific stub, depending on the target object. The ORB interface supports direct client interactions with ORB, and the skeleton is specific to the interface and object adapter. In turn, the object adapter skeleton gets services of ORB through OA.

The IDL (Interface Definition Language) is highlighted in the bottom part of Figure 4–4. The IDL describes interfaces that a client object calls. It is used to describe operations and operation parameters.

IDL mappings to C are part of CORBA, and IDL uses the same rules as C++, but is more restrictive. Like CMIP, types, inheritance, attributes, names, and scoping are included in the IDL operations.

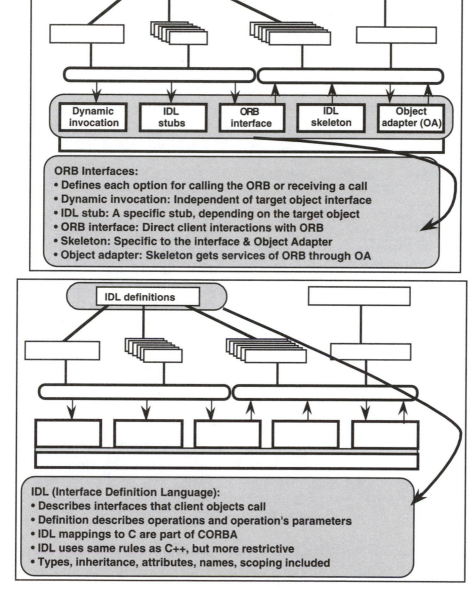

Figure 4–4   CORBA: Interfaces and IDL definitions.

The interface repository (IR) (top part of Figure 4–5) contains objects that represent IDL at run time; it can use objects that have not been previously compiled. It also contains other information, such as debuggers. Stubs provides user access from IDL and makes calls to an ORB. Skeletons provides services specific to an interface and a language. The information repository allows to ORB to locate and activate implementations of objects.

The ORB is defined by its interfaces and with other components (bottom part of Figure 4–5). It provides a set of services to a client. The ORB core provides basic representation of objects and communications of requests, the other services tailored to fit the needs of the user.

TMN

Objectives

Like most of ITU-T's recommendations on models, the TMN is a generic model that describes the functions, interfaces, and reference points of a management system. In this case, TMN is organized around OSI concepts, insofar as possible. TMN also is organized around object-oriented techniques, which makes it supportive of CMIP and CMISE. In addition, TMN employs the five management functional areas of OSI: security management, performance management, accounting management, configuration management, and fault management.

The TMN specifications are published by ITU-T in the M.3010 documents. TMN, with the use of the concepts just described, provides the framework for modeling management services in any type of network. TMN development has been going on for over a decade. The efforts first began in 1985 with an ITU Study Group IV. Then, in 1988, the Blue Books included M.30, which was a precursor to Recommendation M.3010.

The objectives of TMN are to:

- Provide a framework (a generic model) for management
- Describe the appropriate functions that exist in the parts of the TMN
- Define the interfaces between the TMN and the actual networks
- Make use of OSI-based services, where appropriate
- Employ the object-oriented approach to represent TMN architecture
- Employ the OSI five management functional areas (X.700)

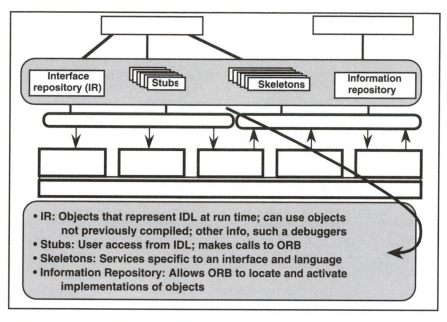

• IR: Objects that represent IDL at run time; can use objects
  not previously compiled; other info, such a debuggers
• Stubs: User access from IDL; makes calls to ORB
• Skeletons: Services specific to an interface and language
• Information Repository: Allows ORB to locate and activate
  implementations of objects

Interface
repository (IR)

Stubs

Skeletons

Information
repository

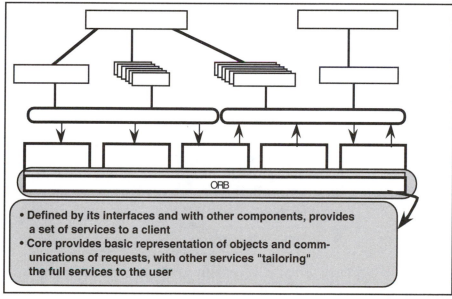

• Defined by its interfaces and with other components, provides
  a set of services to a client
• Core provides basic representation of objects and communications of requests, with other services "tailoring"
  the full services to the user

ORB

Figure 4–5   CORBA: IRs, stubs, skeletons, and CORE.

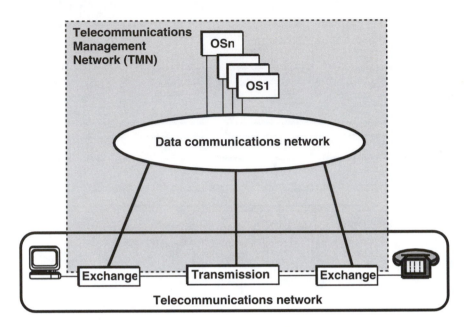

Figure 4–6 Telecommunications Management Network (TMN).

TMN defines the major functions of a management network and the interfaces between these functions and the user equipment. As Figure 4–6 illustrates, TMN defines operations at the exchange and at the transmission system levels, between the TMN network and the user devices, as well as between different vendors' operations systems (OSs). The X.700 Recommendations are considered to be a subset of TMN. Additionally, TMN is a separate network and is logically distinct from the networks that are being managed.

Function Blocks

The TMN architecture is organized around TMN functions (and function blocks). These function blocks describe the activities that TMN performs in its management responsibilities. The function blocks are also further organized into functional components. Any pair of function blocks that exchange information between them are separated by reference points (much like the ITU-T ISDN reference model).

Figure 4–7 shows the function blocks that are directly related to the management operations of TMN. The exchange of management information is provided by the functional blocks and reference points. The circles

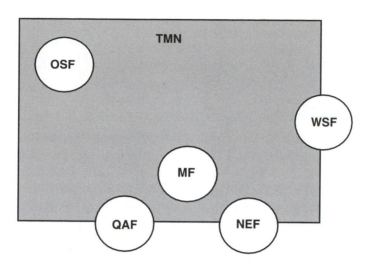

where:

OSF	Operations systems function
MF	Mediation function
WSF	Workstation function
QAF	Q adapter function
NEF	Network element function

Figure 4–7   TMN function blocks.

in the figure symbolize the functions—some of which are not completely in the TMN (explained below).

The function blocks are responsible for the following :

- *Operations Systems Function (OSF) block:* Provides overall management responsibilities for the entire TMN. It includes management functions of the TMN and communicates with network element functions (NEF), described next.
- *Network Element Function (NEF) block:* Communicates with TMN in order to allow the managed network to be managed. Responsible for representing the managed functions to the TMN; as such these functions are not part of TMN.
- *Workstation Function (WSF) block:* Acts as the interface to the human user, and as such, part of it operates outside of the TMN.
- *Mediation Function (MF) block*: Acts as a converter for convergence operator between an OSF and NEF (or a QAF) in the event that these function blocks have some differences that need to be resolved.

- *Q Adapter Function (QAF) block*: Acts as a converter between TMN functions and non-TMN functions that are somewhat similar to NEF and OSF. It translates between a TMN reference point and a proprietary reference point.

Reference Points

The TMN uses reference points to delineate the boundaries between function blocks. Like other ITU-T communications models, these reference points serve to identify the information that is transferred between function blocks. So, the reference point is an interface.

Figure 4–8 shows three classes of reference points, which are called TMN reference points. Two other reference points are defined (not shown in this figure), which are called non-TMN reference points.

The q reference point exists between OSF, QAF, MF, and NEF. The f reference point exists between WSF. The x reference point exists between OSFs of two TMNs. The x reference point can also exist between a TMN OSF and an entity in a non-TMN that performs OSF-type opera-

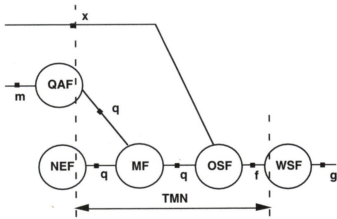

where:

OSF	Operations systems function
MF	Mediation function
WSF	Workstation function
QAF	Q adapter function
NEF	Network element function
q	Reference point class between OSF, MF, QAF, and NEF
f	Reference point class for attachment of WSF
x	Reference point class between OSFs

Figure 4–8   TMN reference points.

tions. The two other reference points are g and m. The g reference point exists between a WSF and end users. The m reference point exists between a QAF and managed entities that are not TMN-compliant.

These reference points define the protocol suites and the protocol messages that are used to exchange information between TMN functions. The interfaces are based on object-oriented concepts. Therefore, the messages exchanged at the reference points are concerned with objects and object manipulations. Objects are defined at the reference points, as well as the valid operations for each reference point.

Figure 4–9 shows two major pieces of TMN: the data communications functions (DCF) and the message communications functions (MCF). The DCF is tasked with providing the transport/bearer services, which includes the typical functions of the OSI physical, data link, and network layers. TMN places no specific requirement on the actual protocols that reside in DCF. Consequently, these services can be provided with X.25, MANs, SS#7, or the data communications channel (DCC) fields of SONET.

The MCF is associated with any of the TMN functional blocks that have a physical interface. Its purpose is to exchange management information with peer entities. It consists of protocol stacks that allow the communication of the function blocks to DCF. It may also provide protocol convergence services, if necessary.

Figure 4–10 provides an example of how the various function blocks can be interconnected with the reference points. From the perspective of TMN, an interface is based on the reference point, although physical in-

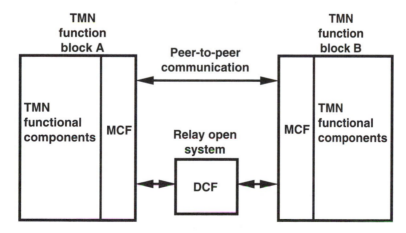

Figure 4–9 Data communications functions (DCF) and the message communications functions (MCF) roles.

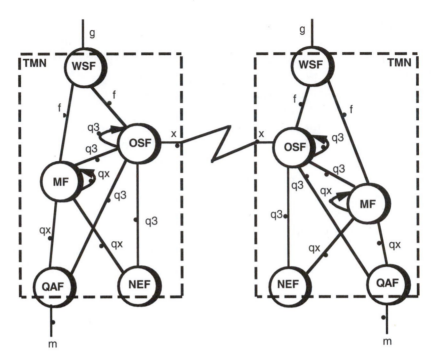

Figure 4–10   Function blocks and reference points.

terfaces may not be visible since reference points may be contained within equipment.

The q reference points are used to separate the flow of information between function blocks. As a general rule, function blocks using the q reference points may not support the full services of the TMN reference model. Additionally, the q reference points are defined between certain sets of the function blocks as shown in this figure.

The f reference points are located only between the WSF and OSF function blocks and/or the WSF and MF function blocks.

The x reference points are located only between the OSF function blocks residing in different TMNs.

The g reference points are located outside a TMN boundary. This is considered an interface between a WSF and a human user. TMN does not define the operations at this reference point but information is available in the Z.300 series. Likewise, the m reference points are located outside the TMN between the QAF and non-TMN entities.

The TMN defines operations between managed objects and managed resources in accordance with common OSI practices and the X.700 recommendations (see Figure 4–11). As such, the managing system operates

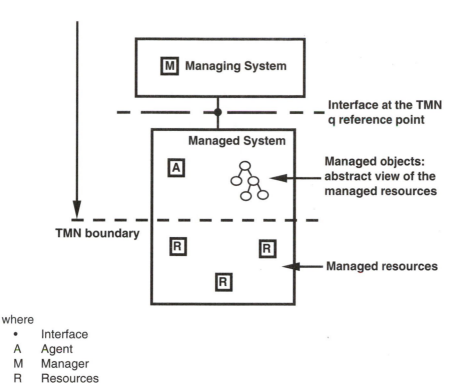

where
- • Interface
- A Agent
- M Manager
- R Resources

Figure 4–11 Managed objects and managed resources.

with the managed system across a q reference point that delineates the logical information exchange between these function blocks. In an actual implementation, the operations between the managing system and the agent are invoked through the common management information protocol (CMIP) and the common management information services element (CMISE) (Recommendations X.711 and X.710). In the spirit of TMN and the OSI Model in general, the aspects of the actual managed resources are beyond the TMN boundary.

An Example of TMN Architecture

Figure 4–12 shows one example of a TMN architecture—somewhat simplified, but certainly illustrative of a functioning model. The operations system (OS) performs the OSFs; it may also provide MFs, QAFs, and WSFs. The mediation device (MD) performs MFs and may also provide OSFs, QAFs, and WSFs. The Q adapter (QA) connects network elements (NEs) or OSs with non-TMN compatible interfaces (that is to say,

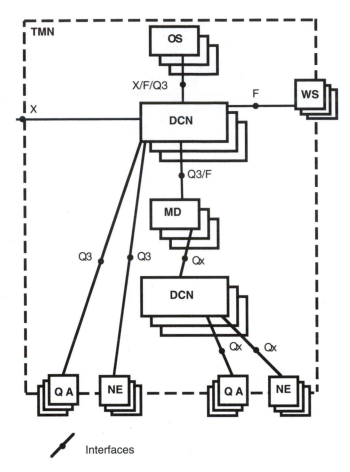

Figure 4–12   Simplified TMN architecture.

m reference points to qx or q3 interfaces). The data communication network (DCN) operates at OSI layers 1, 2, and 3 and supports the DCF. The workstation (WS) is responsible for performing WSFs. The WS must translate information at the f reference point for display at a g reference point and vice versa.

TYING THE PIECES TOGETHER

TMN uses the conventional manager/agent concept for the exchange of messages between functions: The manager issues management messages and receives notifications, and the agent manages the managed objects, receives messages (directions) from the manager, and emits notifications to the manager.

In Figure 4–13, the manager and agent between systems A, B, and C are part of the TMN. The operations between the manager and the agent in system B are not part of the TMN. Further, the actual resources are not part of the TMN, but their view, through the information model, is part of TMN. System A manages system B by referencing the information model B, and system B manages system C by the information model C.

The situation in which an entity manages another entity, which manages yet another entity, is called the cascading of systems. So, a system can be both a manager and an agent.

As discussed further in Chapter 8, CMIP is the layer 7 network management protocol that is used to exchange the network management

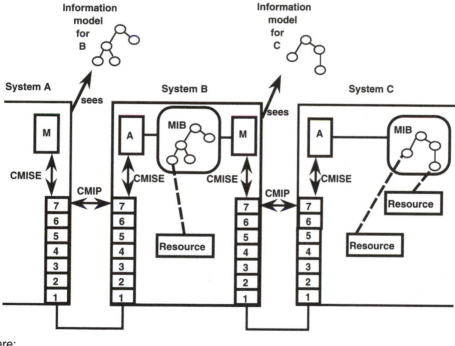

where:
    MIB   Managament information base
    M   Manager
    A   Agent
    CMIP   Common management information protocol
    CMISE   Common management information service element

Figure 4–13   Interworking TMN functions.

messages between the manager and agent. CMISE is the OSI-based service definition that defines the interface between the CMIP software and the manager/agent software.

The management information base (MIB) is an important part of TMN. The MIB identifies the network elements (managed objects). It also contains the unambiguous names that are to be associated with each managed object.

From the conceptual viewpoint, MIBs are really quite simple. Yet, if they are not implemented properly, the network management protocols (such as CMIP) are of little use. These network management protocols rely on the MIB to define the managed objects in the network. As shown in Figure 4–13, the MIB is used by the agent to present a view of the network resources to the manager.

It should be emphasized that the MIB represents the managed objects and is not the actual network resources; that is, the MIB is a database that contains information about the managed objects. For example, a MIB can contain information about the number of packets that have been sent and received across an X.25 interface; it can contain statistics on the number of connections that exist on a TCP port, and so on.

The MIB defines the contents of the information that are carried with the network management protocols, such as CMIP. It also contains information that describes the manager's ability to access elements of the MIB. For example, manager A might have read-only capabilities to a MIB while another manager may have read/write capabilities.

Network management protocols (with few exceptions) do not operate directly on the managed object, they operate on the MIB. In turn, the MIB is the reflection of the managed object. How this reflection is conveyed is a proprietary decision. The important aspect of the MIB is that it defines the (1) elements that are managed, (2) how the user accesses them, and (3) how they can be reported.

The MIB is usually written in an OSI-based layer 6 language, called Abstract Syntax Notation One (ASN.1). ASN.1 defines the structure and contents of the network management message. Since the MIB contains the elements that are managed as well as their names, the network management software can access the MIB for guidance on how to formulate the network management message.

The OSI and TMN architecture describe the identification scheme and structure for the managed objects in the MIB. The objects within an TMN have many common characteristics across subnetworks, vendor products, and individual components. It would be quite wasteful for each organization to spend precious resources and time in coding ASN.1 to describe these resources. Therefore, the MIB provides a registration scheme wherein objects can be defined and categorized within a registration hierarchy.

SUMMARY

The intelligent network architecture is based on common software and reusable software programs. As such, CORBA and object-oriented MIBs are valuable tools to manage the IN system components. In addition, TMN provides a model that is supportive of and complementary to the IN.

5

The Bellcore and ITU-T Call Model Operations

This chapter describes the operations of the Bellcore AIN and the ITU-T IN call models. The models are similar and most major AIN/IN vendors support both specifications. The goal of this chapter is to present the major concepts and operations of the models. They are detailed enough to allow a programmer to design software modules from them.[1] That level of detail is best left to the specifications themselves. The general reader is likely not concerned with the nuances of each model anyway, but for the vendor who is after more precise information, I will be careful to explain in each section of this chapter which model is under discussion.

I have made the point in earlier chapters of the importance of having a formal method for the IN service creation operations. In this part of the book, we will discuss an example of how a model is created and examine some tools for supporting this model.

THE CALL MODEL PROCEDURES

The call model is a representation of a sequence of procedures executed by an IN to set up, manage, and clear an IN session between IN

---

[1]I was pleasantly surprised, upon reading these models, that they were not "abstract" like most models published by the standards organizations.

components. It allows both ends of a session, regardless of the specific vendor's machine, to share a common view of the ongoing phases and operations of the IN operation. In simple words, it defines the interfaces, states, and events that are associated with each type IN service.

To emphasize these ideas of the IN, the call model:

- Provides a simple description for IN calls that is independent of switch type or manufacturer's architecture.
- Depicts in an unambiguous manner the states and events that should be visible to IN machines, but not states and events that are specific to a vendor's architecture.
- From the first two aspects: Provides an environment for the fast creation of services, independent of vendor-specific architectures.

ITU-T IN Services

The ITU-T has defined a number of services that are supported by the IN. These services are classified as type A and type B services. Type A services involve no interactions of the SCPs to support a service and entail one set of parties, typically the calling and called party. Type B services may involve multiple customers and may require the interaction of several SCPs. CS-1 supports only type A services in order to reduce the complexity of the IN.

Table 5–1 provides a summary of the CS-1 services. Each service is identified with two to four letters.

Table 5–1 ITU-T IN Services

Service	Description
Abbreviated dialing (ABD)	Allows subscriber to use fewer numbers (digits) when dialing a called party
Account card calling (ACC)	Calls can be made from any telephone and charged to one specific account
Automatic alternative billing (AAB)	Calls can be made from any telephone and charged to an account, regardless of the called or calling party line
Call completion to busy subscriber (CCBS)	Caller to a busy line is allowed to stay on hold until the line is free (without making a new call)
Call distribution (CD)	Incoming calls can be routed to another line, based on user requirements

(continued)

Table 5–1 *Continued*

Service	Description
Call forwarding (CF)	Subscriber can inform network to forward an incoming call to another line
Call rerouting distribution (CRD)	Reroutes incoming calls to a predefined line if the called line is busy
Conference calling (CON)	Multiple parties can participate in a call
Credit card calling (CCC)	Call is charged to a specific credit card
Destination call routing (DCR)	Routes calls based on time, origin, calling party
Freephone (FPH)	Supports free calls (800/888 service)
Follow-me diversion (FMD)	Allows calls to "follow" a party by redirecting calls to other locations
Malicious call ID (MCI)	Incoming calls can be logged and identified
Mass calling (MAS)	Subscriber can obtain statistics on high-volume call-ins (to one or several numbers)
Originating call screening (OCS)	Outgoing calls can be barred, based on an examination of the calling and/or called number
Premium rate (PRM)	Operators can offer certain rates to obtain revenue; usually, revenue is shared between two service providers/operators
Security screening (SEC)	A closed user group feature in which the calling party may not be allowed to access a called party number
Selective call forwarding (SCF)	For a busy or no answer, preselected callers are rerouted
Split charging (SPL)	Calling and called party share in the expense of the call
Terminating call screening (TCS)	Subscriber can specify a list (screen) that identifies which incoming calls are to be accepted or rejected (do not disturb)
Televoting (VOT)	Subscriber can vote, respond to polls, give opinions by dialing into permanent or temporary numbers
Universal access number (UAN)	Several terminating lines are dialed with one number
Universal personal telecomm (UPT)	All incoming user lines are accessible by one particular number, regardless of the location of the user
User-defined routing (UDR)	Customer can establish routes for calls that customer originates
Virtual private network (VPN)	Subscriber is given part of the bandwidth of a public network, with the performance of a private network

BELLCORE BASIC CALL MODEL

The following material provides a description of the Bellcore AIN call model. As a brief iteration of points covered in Chapter 2, Bellcore's AIN is consistent with ITU-T's IN.

Point-in-Call (PIC)

As depicted in Figure 5–1, the Bellcore model is a high-level finite state machine, and is organized around actions or a collection of actions called a point-in-call (PIC). The PIC represents the external view of the AIN operations. By external, I mean that the AIN implementor is free to choose the method of implementation for the actual software, just as long as the software behaves according to this external representation. However, each vendor is required to support the interfaces depicted by the PICs. As Figure 5–1 shows, a PIC is described by an entry point and an exit point. We shall see shortly that the PIC contains other information at these points.

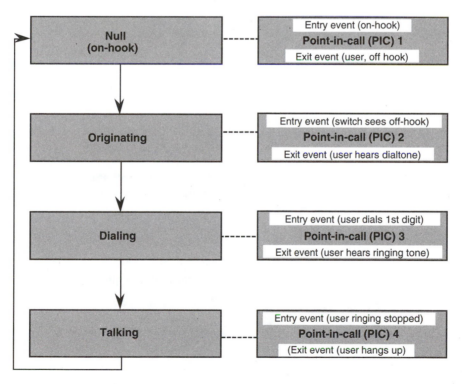

Figure 5–1   Example of basic call model (BCM).

Detection Points (DPs)

Detection points (DPs) operate between the PICs. They delineate the points in the model where call processing is suspended and other actions invoked; for example, the action of sending a message to another node. Query messages are associated with specific DPs. When a specific query message is received by a node, it knows the exact stage of a call that has been completed in the transmitting node. As Figure 5–2 illustrates, the DP is located between PICs (acting as transition points) in the call model.

Triggers

DPs are associated with triggers. A trigger lists a set of criteria that contain a condition or conditions that must be satisfied before a message is generated. In addition, the trigger point must include the address of the node that is to receive the message if it is generated. Trigger criteria are either satisfied or not satisfied.

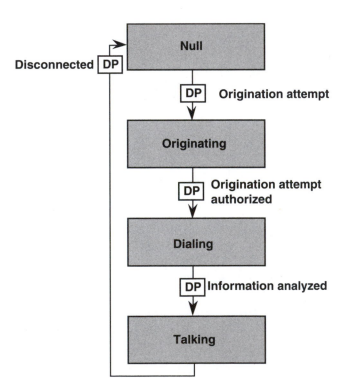

Figure 5–2   Example of detection points (DPs).

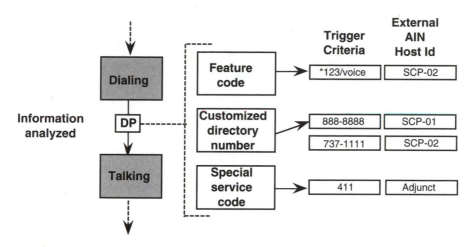

Figure 5–3   Detection points and triggers.

As Figure 5–3 shows, DPs can consist of one to many operations and their associated triggers. A combination of the DP and trigger criteria, if satisfied, results in the suspension of call processing at the node. The suspension results in the creation and sending of a message to the relevant recipient node and operations remain suspended until a response is returned from the remote node. If none of the trigger criteria are satisfied, call processing proceeds directly to the next PIC.

Originating and Terminating Models

The call model is divided into two parts: the originating call model (OCM), and the terminating call model (TCM). Both models describe a state machine for the call processing logic. As Figure 5–4 depicts, the OCM and TCM operate in the AIN node. An AIN operation begins with the invocation of the OCM, then the TCM is started based on the satisfaction of trigger criteria. Once the TCM starts, both the OCM and TCM operate in parallel, although the specific instance of the OCM may be suspended when the TCM is operating.

The OCM initiates the call, performs call validation of the calling party, and is responsible for controlling the call to its completion. The TCM validates the called party and is responsible for terminating the call.

I made the point earlier that both the OCM and TCM can operate in an AIN node. Consequently, if a customer call involves the operations of more than one AIN node, both models are active in both nodes (see Figure 5–5). The majority of the operations will occur as follows:

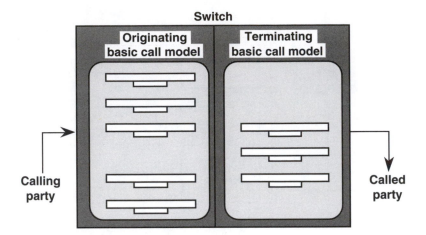

Figure 5–4   Originating and terminating basic call model.

- The switch serving the calling party executes most of the OCM logic.
- The switch serving the called party executes most of the TCM logic.

Examples of AIN Operations

We learned earlier in this book that the call model defines the exchange of information between an SSP and an SCP. As Figure 5–6 depicts, an incoming call is processed through the originating call model (OCM) module by executing the state logic with points in call (PICs) and detection points (DPs). This figure shows the four basic events to execute the model leading to the invocation of trigger operations. In event 1, the SSP receives information (i.e., dialed digits, E.164 addresses, etc.). It exe-

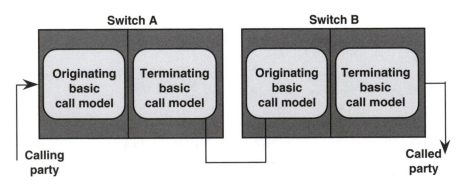

Figure 5–5   The call model at multiple switches.

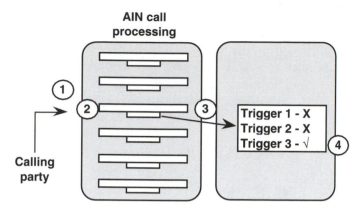

Figure 5–6   Matching a trigger.

cutes the PICs until (for example) the information analyzed detection point is reached, which invokes the trigger logic (depicted in event 3). The various trigger criteria are analyzed and, in event 4, trigger 3 and its criteria are satisfied.

Based on satisfying the trigger 3 criteria, the AIN node assembles the required information to build a query message, as depicted in Figure 5–7. This message contains all the fields necessary to identify the message (addresses, type of message, etc.). In event 6, this message is coded

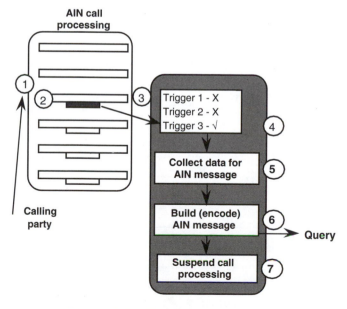

Figure 5–7   Sending the query.

into the SS7 TCAP query message and sent to the relevant SCP. After the query is sent, event 7 shows that the SSP suspends call processing on this particular call to await the response from the SCP node.

The operations at the SCP are straightforward. In event 8, Figure 5–8, the SCP decodes the incoming TCAP message. Based on the analysis of the fields in the message, it executes the specific software module to service the query (event 9). This module executes the operation and generates the parameters that are used to create the response message (event 10). Finally, in event 11 the SCP creates a TCAP response message and sends this message to the originating SSP.

When the response arrives at the SSP, the suspended call is activated (see Figure 5–9). The message is decoded as depicted in event 12, which may entail the execution of other actions (such as "do not charge for this call," "replace the dialed number with a different number," etc.). The information processed in event 12 also instructs the SCP where it should begin the activation of the call processing. In some instances, it may assume processing at a different point in the call than is shown in the sequential state diagram. The activation of a different PIC is called *warping*. Whatever the case, processing is resumed as illustrated in event 13.

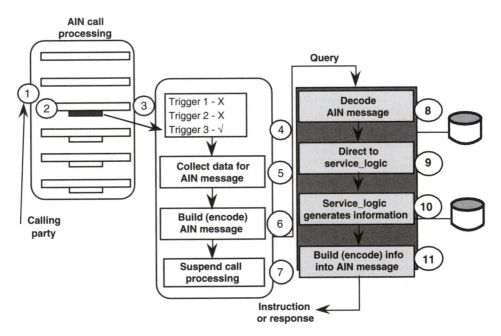

Figure 5–8   The node responds.

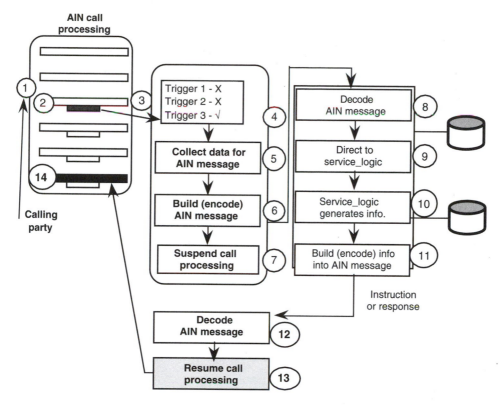

Figure 5–9   Processing resumes at query site.

PICs and DPs

Figure 5–10 represents the PICs and DPs in the originating call model (of Bellcore AIN 0.1). For the PICs:

- *Null:* Line or trunk interface is idle (no call exists), and switch provides supervision.
- *Authorizing origination attempt:* Switch verifies authority of the user to place a call with the given properties (e.g., line restrictions). Any glare situation detected is resolved.
- *Collecting information:* Switch collects initial information (e.g., service codes, address information) from user according to a specified dialing plan.
- *Analyzing information:* Switch interprets and translates the collected information according to the specified numbering plan, determining the called party ID, type of call, carrier, and route index.

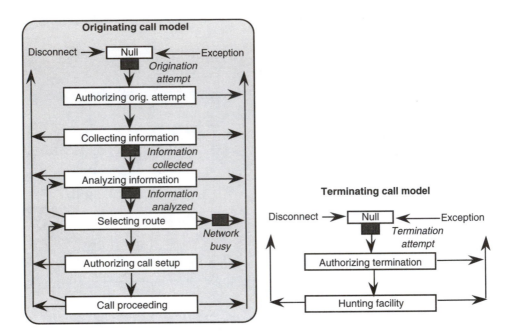

Figure 5–10   The originating basic call model.

- *Selecting route:* Switch interprets the analysis results to select the outgoing route (e.g., point to a local DN, point to a list of trunk names).
- *Authorizing call setup:* Switch verifies that the calling party is authorized to place the call (e.g., checks toll restrictions).
- *Call proceeding:* Originating-call portion notifies terminating-call portion of desire to terminate on a DN or on a trunk group name.

For the DPs:

- *Origination attempt:* Used for situations where a message is to be sent to the SCP as soon as user goes off hook (hot line type services).
- *Information collected:* Used for situations (1) where a message is to be sent to the SCP unless an escape code is dialed, or (2) for incoming trunk receiving only public DNs.
- *Information analyzed:* Used for situations where the type of digits dialed (feature code, public DN, special service code) must be ascertained before message can be sent to SCP.
- *Network busy:* Used to send message to SCP requesting overflow routes (when all routes known to SSP are busy).

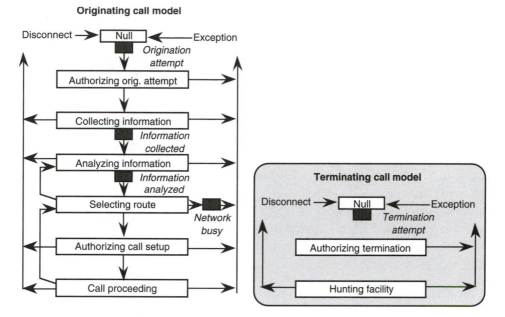

Figure 5–11   The terminating basic call model.

Figure 5–11 depicts the PICs and DPs in terminating call model (AIN 0.1). For the PICs:

- *Null:* Line or trunk interface is idle (no call exists) and switch provides supervision.
- *Authorizing origination:* Switch verifies authority to route this call to the terminating access (e.g., check business group restrictions).
- *Hunting facility:* The busy/idle status of the terminating access of the call is determined.

And for the DPs:

- *Termination attempt:* Used in situations where a message is to be sent to the SCP before the SSP attempts to terminate the call.

THE ITU-T IN MODEL

The ITU-T call model is similar to the Bellcore model just discussed. The major difference is that the Bellcore AIN specifications are not built on the INCM, discussed in Chapter 3.

At this juncture, I am going to focus on the ITU-T model again for one reason: to bring our analysis back to the IN planes of the INCM that were introduced in Chapter 3 (see Figure 3–1).

Point of Initiation (POI) and Point of Return (POR)

The discussions in Chapter 3 explained the use of point of initiation (POI) and point of return (POR) operations. Recall that whenever the basic call processing is not able to provide a requested service, it invokes the global service logic (GSL), as shown in Figure 5–12. This invocation occurs in the basic call processing at the point of initiation (POI). The execution is then turned over to GSL, which executes a chain of SIBs, after which it returns to the BCP at the POR.

The POIs and PORs specified in the ITU-T CS-1 are discussed next. They are similar to the Bellcore point-in-call (PICs) described earlier. First, the POIs:

- *Call originated:* Describes that the customer has made a service request but has not specified a destination address. For example, the customer has gone off-hook, but has not dialed a number.
- *Address collected:* Describes that the customer has presented the dialed address to the network.
- *Address analyzed:* Describes that the dialed address has been analyzed.
- *Call arrival:* Describes that the network has received the signals necessary to try a completion of the call to the called party.
- *Busy:* Describes that the called party is busy.
- *No answer:* Describes that the called party did not answer.

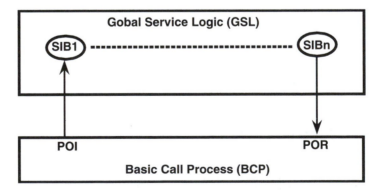

Figure 5–12   Example of point of initiation (POI) and point of return (POR) operations.

- *Call acceptance:* Describes that the call process is still active. The end-to-end connection is not fixed yet. For example, the called party has answered, but the connection has not been completely switched through.
- *Active state:* Describes that the call is active. It also indicates that the end-to-end is set up and operational.
- *End of call:* Describes that a party is now disconnected.

And next, the PORs:

- *Continue with existing data:* Describes that the BCP should proceed with call processing operations without any changes furnished by the SCP.
- *Proceed with new data:* Describes that the BCP should proceed with call processing operations with data revisions.
- *Handle as transit:* Describes that the call should be restarted at the initial BCP state.
- *Clear call :* Describes that the call is to be cleared by the BCP.
- *Enable call party handling:* Describes that the BCP to handle multiple parties (this POR is "for further study").
- *Initiate call:* Describes that the call should be started (even if there is no POI, in which case the GSL starts the call).

SIB Identifiers

In order to identify SIBs, a four-digit convention is used to identify the FE, the SIB, and FEAs that are common to FEs and SIBs. The rules for this number are:

Value is XYYZ
where x = FE
YY = SIB section number
Z distinguishes FEAs that have a common XYY

As examples, a SIB to connect to resource is number 2073, the play announcement SIB is 3071, and the disconnect forward connection is 2077. Figure 5–13 shows some examples of the information flows between FEAs. This SIB is the QUEUE SIB (07). As stated earlier, these information flows are actually INAP operations. This example shows three information flows: (1) connect to resource (CONN.TO.RES), (2) play announcement (PLAY.ANN), and (3) disconnect forward connection (DISC.FWD.CONN).

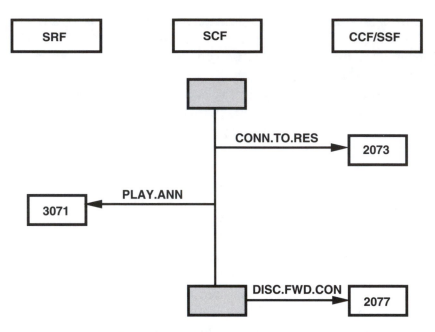

Figure 5–13   Example information flows. *(Source:* **Conference on Intelligent Networks, May 9, 1996, London, IBC Technical Services Ltd, and ITU-T Q.1214).**

Figure 5–14 continues the example in Figure 5–13 with a specific service called automatic alternative billing (AAB). This service allows the user to make a call from any telephone and charge the call to an account specific to the service. The distinction with AAB is that the charged call has nothing to do with the calling or called address. Service is executed by signing an account code append to the service unit.

To invoke AAB, a customer dials a predetermined access code (which is a free call). Different access codes may be used to identify the language that is to be used during the process. The customer receives announcements informing him or her to dial the person's account number, including the PIN. Once these values have been entered and validated, a check might be made for the account credit.

The AAB service also allows a calling party to call another party and ask this party to receive the call at the called party expense (obviously, call collect). The sequence of the SIB executions are listed below, in relation to the POI and POR with nine events. In event 1 a standardized address analyzed POI signifies that the called digits have been analyzed and AIN services are to be invoked. GSL SIBs are invoked as follows (these SIB numbers are for this example only, and are not part of the standards):

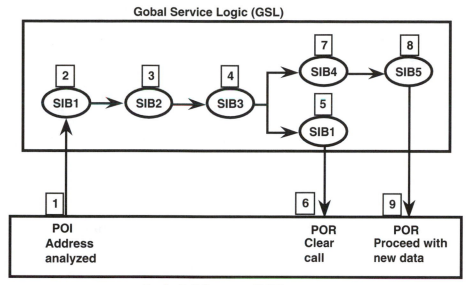

Figure 5–14 The IN model in operation with the SIBs—
example is automatic alternative billing (AAB).

- SIB 1 (User Interaction SIB): Supports the exchange of information between the user and the AIN (to/from the basic call process).
- SIB 2 (Verify): Essentially, an editor that verifies that the user data is syntactically correct.
- SIB 3 (Screen): Checks if the user data (for example, a telephone number) is stored in the screen list. If it is found, the IN service proceeds to the Translate SIB. If not found, the User Interaction SIB is invoked, and the call is cleared.
- SIB 4 (Translate): This SIB is the focal point of this process. It ascertains the correct output data from the input data. In this example (automatic alternative billing), the user is charged for the call, regardless of the calling line or the called line.
- SIB 5 (Charge): This SIB resolves the account to which the call is to be charged.

Finally, the POR Proceed With New Data is entered, and the call is processed with the new information.

ASN.1 Code for Connect to Resource

The ASN.1 code for connect to resource is shown in Figure 5–15. In this example, the parameters, arguments, and errors that are included in this particular information flow connect a call from the SSP to an IP with the SRF. The connect to resource argument is a SEQUENCE type with an imbedded CHOICE type, as illustrated in this figure. I have not included all the ASN.1 code to make this a complete stand-alone example, but enough to give you an idea of the composition of ASN.1.

Modeling with the Specification and Description Language (SDL)

In order to define and explain a system as complex as an IN, it is necessary to have a means to describe its detailed operations. The SDL specifications from the ITU-T are used by many IN development teams to meet this necessity, and this section provides an example of the use of SDL.

```
ConnectToResource ::= OPERATION
      ARGUMENT
          ConnectToResourceArg
      ERRORS {
          MissingParameter
          SystemFailure
          TaskRefused
          UnexpectedComponentSequence
          UnexpectedDataValue
          UnexpectedParameter
          }

ConnectToResourceArg ::= SEQUENCE {
      CHOICE {
          ipRoutingAddress        [0] IPRoutingAddress
          legid                   [1] Legid
          both                    [2] SEQUENCE {
                      ipRoutingAddress        [0] IPRoutingAddress
                      legid                   [1] Legid
                      }
          none                    [3[ NULL
          }}
```

Figure 5–15   ASN.1 code for connect to resource.

Many companies favor the use of SDL for the following reasons:

- Operations are depicted with graphical notations
- Operations are based on finite state machine theory, which is a good tool for describing distributed processing systems, such as an IN (see Chapter 4)
- Tools can be created to validate an SDL-based IN specification
- Prototype models can be automatically produced from an SDL chart and code can be produced by the "press of a button"

An SDL system is a set of blocks that are connected together. One or more processes exist within the blocks. In effect, SDL uses many conventional flow charting concepts. The SDL specification is over 700 pages (including annexes to Z.100 and Z.110). It is beyond our analysis to cover SDL in detail, but Figure 5–16 shows some of the major aspects of SDL.

The DSL example in Figure 5–17 shows the logic for checking a called party number at the initial DP and taking one of three actions, depending upon the value of the number. If the number indicates the 700 service is in use, a query is sent to a database (db_nt_request), the call is suspended, and a timer is started to await a reply (Start (wfDbTimer). Activity is started again upon receiving a reply (to (sf_nt_resp)).

If the service is not in use, a connection is made to the resource to play an announcement and release the call. Otherwise, the call is released.

C CODE AND SDL

Figure 5–18 shows the code in C that was written based on the SDL in the previous figure.[2] You might wish to correlate the two together. The code is well-written with comments. Once again, this information was from the Conference on Intelligent Networks, May 9, 1996, sponsored by IBC Technical Services Ltd. I thank my friends at IBC for furnishing this information, and Olli Martikainen, who conducted the presentation.

---

[2] Earlier, I made the point that the call models were detailed enough from which to develop software modules. This capability is provided through SDL and AIN.1, which are part of the IN Standards. Of course the code must still be written, as Olli Martikainen demonstrates, but tools are available to automate the process.

- Describes the operations and behaviors of a telecommunications system
- Used with timers to govern the system's actions
- Examples of SDL symbols:

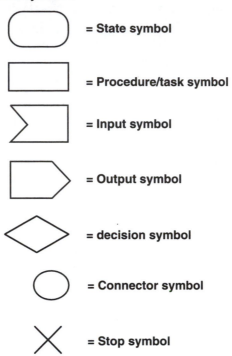

= State symbol

= Procedure/task symbol

= Input symbol

= Output symbol

= decision symbol

= Connector symbol

= Stop symbol

Figure 5–16   Specification and description language (SDL).

EXAMPLES OF SERVICES TO THE USER

In Chapter 1, an example was provided of how the AIN (returning to the Bellcore example) can insulate a customer from the physical locations of the parties of called numbers—the example was to order a pizza. Recall that a customer dialed a number for any Pizza-a-Go-Go outlet in a metropolitan area. The dialed number triggered the invocation of AIN operations, and the originating SSP was given the telephone number of the nearest Pizza-a-Go-Go store.

The operations to support this service in the Bellcore AIN model are shown in Figure 5–19. After the information is collected and analyzed, the information analyzed trigger detection point is reached. The called digits are compared to specific criteria (conditions) (called the Specific_Digit_String trigger. The match causes the SSP to suspend the call processing and send an Information_Analyzed query message (containing the calling and called party numbers) to the SCP.

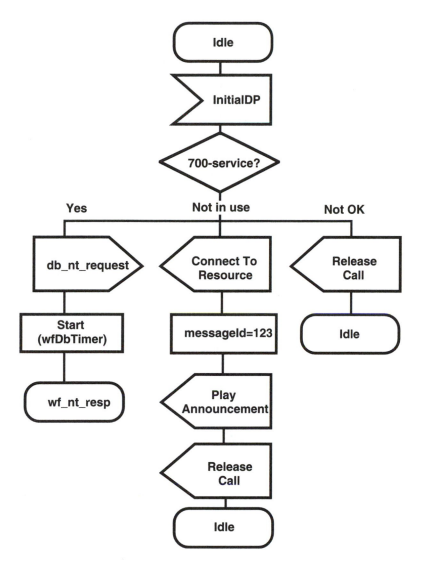

Figure 5–17 Example of SDL coding for an IN service.
(Source: **Conference on Intelligent Networks, May 9, 1996, London, IBC Technical Services Ltd.)**

The SCP searches the database for the record of the called party number, correlates this number with the calling party number, and sends a Forward_DN message back to the SSP. This message tells the SSP to connect the call to the nearest Pizza-a-Go-Go location.

We also looked at an AIN example of the do not disturb feature. Figure 5–20 continues the discussion and shows the operations in relation to the AIN model. As we learned earlier, the AIN subscriber goes off-hook

```
(* CVOPS state-automation for 700-service *)
(* state
        input
            actions *)
idle
    InitialDP {
                (* Call C function that checks
                    calledPartyNumber *)
                result = numberTranslationService( )
                if (result == 700SERVICE) {
                    (* send query to database
                        and await reply *)
                    db_nt_request
                    start (wfDbTimer)
                    to (wf_nt_resp)
                }
                else
                if (result == SERVICE_NOT_IN_USE) {
                    (* Play announcement to user *)
                    ConnectToResource
                    message Id=123
                    PlayAnnouncement
                    ReleaseCall
                    to(idle)
                }
                else {
                    (* error *)
                    ReleaseCall
                    to (idle)
                }
            }
wf_nt_resp
    db_nt_resp                     {
                stop (wfDbTimer)
                if (dbStatus = = OK) {
                    ...
```

Figure 5–18   Coding with C based on the SDL.

and dials the activation digits for the do not disturb feature. The SSP
processes the digits and, when the information analyzed trigger detection
point (TDP) is reached, it is discovered that the caller subscribes to a
trigger at that TDP. The digits are compared against the conditions in
the subscriber AIN trigger, finds a match, and suspends call processing.

The SSP forms an information analyzed query message and sends
this message to the SCP. The message contains the calling number and
the dialed digits.

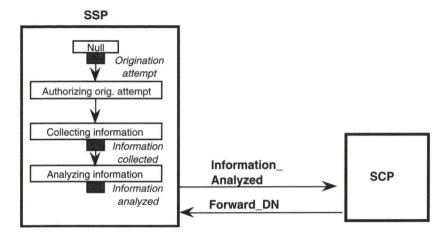

Figure 5–19   AIN dialogue between SSP and SCP: Pizza-a-Go-Go.

The SCP uses the DN to access the subscriber's records and marks the do not disturb service as active.

The SCP then creates a send_to_resource message that instructs the SSP to inform the user of the feature activation with a tone or an announcement.

Figure 5–21 shows the operations for the do not disturb feature, in which a user is allowed to connect to the subscriber. In this example, the SSP collects the dialed digits and identifies the terminating line, recog-

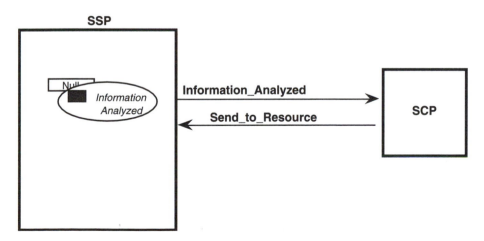

Figure 5–20   AIN dialogue between SSP and SCP: Activate do not disturb feature.

SSP

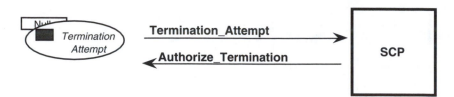

Figure 5–21   AIN dialogue between SSP and SCP: Pass call through.

nizing that this line is marked as an AIN subscriber. The SSP suspends call processing and sends an termination_attempt query message to the SSP. This message contains the calling DN and the called digits.

At the SCP, the called DN is used to access the subscriber's control record where it is ascertained that the do not disturb feature is active. In addition, the associated subscriber list, pertaining to pass-through calls, is checked and a match is found on the calling DN.

The SCP then creates an authorized_termination message and sends it to the SSP. This message directs the SCP to complete the call and the SSP, in turn, connects this caller to the AIN subscriber.

Figure 5–22 shows the do not disturb feature in which a caller is not in the pass-through subscriber list but is allowed to be connected to the AIN customer.

SSP

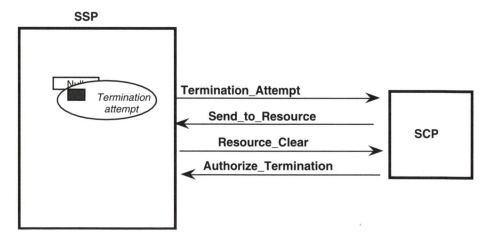

Figure 5–22   AIN dialogue between SSP and SCP: Authorize call termination.

As in the previous example, the SSP recognizes the terminating line in the dialed number as an AIN subscriber and, as before, sends a termination_attempt query message to the SCP. However, the calling party's number is not stored in the customer's control record. Consequently, the SCP creates a send_to_resource message that directs the SSP to play an announcement to the caller and to collect additional digits.

The SSP connects the call to an intelligent peripheral (IP) that is responsible for playing this announcement and collecting the additional digits.

Next, the IP sends a report to the SSP. The SSP sends the additional digits to the SCP in a resource_clear message. The SCP analyzes the dialed digits and discovers that the calling party dialed an authorization code. The SCP then sends the authorized_termination message to the SSP, which, in turn, connects the calling party to the AIN subscriber.

ITU-T BASIC CALL MODEL

As stated earlier, the ITU-T and Bellcore models are quite similar, and use high-level finite state machines. However, the ITU-T model differs slightly from Bellcore's model as shown in Figure 5–23.

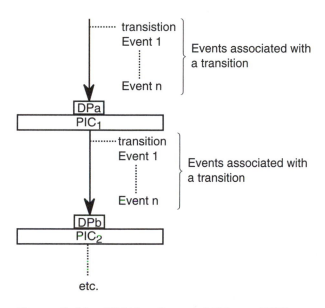

Figure 5–23   ITU-T call model DPs and PICs.

The idea of the ITU-T Basic call state model (BCSM) is that parts of it are not externally visible to IN service logic instances. Those that are visible, are reflected upward to the SSF. These aspects of the BCSM are subject to standardization.

SUMMARY

The call models of Bellcore and the ITU-T are well-constructed tools for the AIN/IN developer. When used with SDL and ASN.1, they are presented in sufficient detail to permit the development of executable code.

6

A More Detailed Analysis of the Bellcore AIN Model

T his chapter provides a more detailed analysis of the Bellcore AIN model 0.1. The PICs and triggers for the originating and terminating modules are the focus of this analysis.

The Bellcore model has undergone a number of changes during the past few years. The most widely-used implementation of the model is based on Bellcore TR-NWT-001284, Advanced Intelligent Network (AIN) 0.1. AIN 0.2 was published next as a revision to AIN 0.1. Finally, in 1996, GR-1298-CORE (AIN Generic Requirements, or AINGR) was published as a major revision to the previous specifications.

The approach in this chapter is to concentrate on AIN 0.1, since it is the standard currently deployed in commercial systems. In the latter part of the chapter, AINGR is introduced and compared to AIN 0.1.

BELLCORE AIN MODEL REVISION (0.1)

The Bellcore basic call model 0.1 was modified in 1992 and now consists of the PICs and PDs shown in Figures 6–1 and 6–2. This model describes the operations that the SSP executes in processing a two-party call. Two tables are used to organize the analysis of the model. Table 6–1 explains each PIC with the following columns in the table:

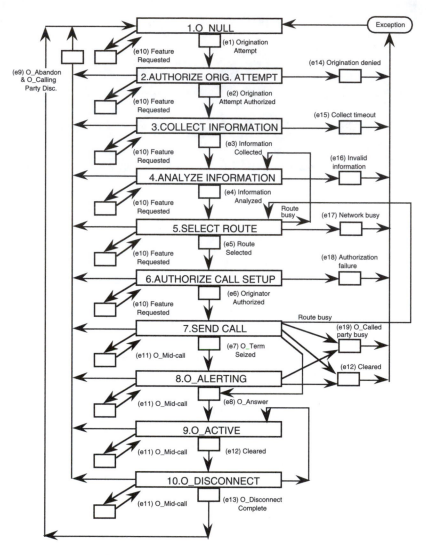

Figure 6–1   Bellcore basic call model.

- Name and number of the PIC
- Entry events(s) for the PIC
- Actions
- Exit event(s) for the PIC

Table 6–2 explains each trigger point with the following columns in the table:

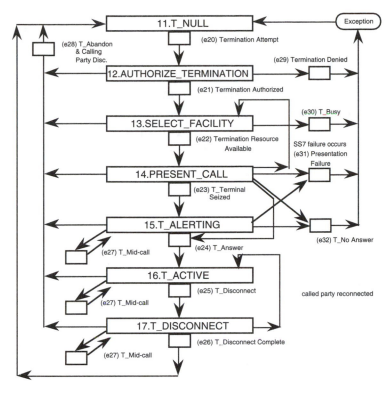

Figure 6–2   Bellcore basic call model (continued).

- Name and number of the trigger event
- Description of the event
- Description of further operations (including messaging)

The joint use of the figures and tables in this chapter is self-explanatory, and I have expanded Bellcore's specification to include tutorial information, which is contained in the tables. Before the tables are examined, a few words are in order about AIN 0.1.

Overview of AIN 0.1

The SSP recognizes a call that requires AIN processing by an SCP but does not make any assumptions about the service that is to be provided. The SSP temporarily suspends the call processing and sends a query to the SCP. In turn, the SCP provides the SSP with information about how to continue the processing of the call.

The AIN 0.1 SSP supports several triggers. In summary, the following list provides the trigger detection point and the associated triggers:

TDP	Triggers
Origination Attempt	Off-Hook Immediate
Info. Collected	Off-Hook Delay
	Channel Setup PRI (Primary Rate Interface)
	Shared Interoffice Trunk
Info. Analyzed	BRI (Basic Rate Interface) Feature Activation Indicator
	Public Feature Code
	Customized Dialing Plan
	3/6/10 Digit
	N11
Network Busy	AFR (Automatic Flexible Routing)
Termination Attempt	Termination Attempt

The following major functions are part of AIN 0.1.

Querying

The SSP is responsible for sending a query to the SCP over an SS7 common channel signaling channel. This query must be sent as a TCAP query message. These query messages correspond to the following TDPs: Origination_Attempt, Info_Collected, Info_Analyzed, Network_Busy, and Termination_Attempt.

Caller Interaction

After receiving the query message from the SSP, the SCP may send back to the SSP a TCAP conversation with permission message. This prompts the SSP to collect additional information from the caller. The caller may send back dial-pulse digits, dual-tone multifrequency (DTMF) signals, or an ISDN information message. Whatever the format of the response, the SSP returns this information back to the SCP in a TCAP conversation package message.

Trigger Activation/Deactivation

The SCP can request the SSP to activate or deactivate certain triggers by sending to the SSP a TCAP query or a TCAP conversation package message. The SSP must respond with either a TCAP response or TCAP conversation package message, respectively. The message indicates if the activation/deactivation was successful.

Response Processing

The SSP, upon receiving a TCAP response message from the SCP, must then take actions such as routing the call, redirecting the call, disconnecting the call, playing an announcement to the caller, and so on. Response processing from the SCP can include the following messages: Analyze_Route, Forward_Call, Send_To_Resource, Authorize_Termination, Disconnect, and Continue.

The SCP response can also indicate that it wishes to be notified when the call ends. If so, this operation is performed with at TCAP unidirectional message.

The SCP may also send the SSP a TCAP Query message which directs it to monitor certain facilities. The facilities are identified in the message and the SSP must report the state of these facilities using a TCAP conversation and response message.

AIN 0.2 NO LONGER USED

The 1996 Bellcore AIN Release stipulates that the term AIN 0.2 is no longer used. Notwithstanding, for purposes of continuity and for those organizations that have been considering its use, this section describes what were originally called AIN 0.2 capabilities—those capabilities beyond AIN 0.1.

Triggering

AIN 0.2 supports four new call processing triggers: O_Called_Party_Busy, O_No_Answer, T_Busy, and T_No_Busy. The purpose of these triggers is to allow the detection of a busy condition on the originating or terminating end and to detect a no answer on the originating or terminating end. In addition, the off-delay trigger from AIN 0.1 is extended to apply to ISDN primary rate interfaces.

Querying

To support the new triggers, several new query messages are defined and some messages defined for AIN 0.1 have had parameters added to them.

Table 6–1   PICs

Name	Entry Event(s)	Action(s)	Exit Event(s)
PIC1 0_Null	Disconnect and clearing of a previous call, after exception handling or system (re)initialization.	Line or trunk interface is idle. Supervision is being provided.	Indication of desire to place outgoing call received from originating party.
PIC2 Authorize Origination Attempt	Indication of desire to place outgoing call received from originating party.	Authority of user to place outgoing call with certain properties (e.g., line restrictions) is being verified.	1. Authority/ability to place outgoing call verified. 2. Authority/ability to place outgoing call denied. 3. Originating party abandons. 4. A feature request is received from the originating party.
PIC3 Collect Information	Authority/ability to place outgoing call is verified.	SSP collects initial information (e.g., dialed address digits) from the user.	1. Availability of complete information from originating party. 2. Information collection error has occurred (e.g., invalid dial string format, digit collection timeout). 3. Originating party abandons call. 4. A feature request is received from calling party.
PIC4 Analyze Information	Availability of complete information from originating party.	SSP interprets and translates information according to the specified numbering plan. Routing address and type of calls (local, long distance) are determined.	1. Availability of routing address and call type. 2. Unable to analyze and translate dial string in the dialing plan. 3. Originating party abandons call. 4. A feature request is received from the originating party.
PIC5 Select Route	1. Availability of routing address and call type. 2. Unable to complete call using specified route (e.g., congestion). Route busy event reported from Call Sent PIC (PIC7).	SSP is interprets the routing address and type of call to select the next route.	1. Terminating resource to which call should be routed has been identified. 2. Unable to select a route (e.g., unable to find a correct route). 3. Originating party abandons call. 4. A feature request is received from the calling party.

Name	Entry Event(s)	Action(s)	Exit Event(s)
PIC6 Authorize Call Setup	Terminating resource to which call should be routed is identified.	SSP verifies the authority of the calling party to place this particular call.	1. Authority of originating party to place this call verified. 2. Authority of originating party to place this call is denied. 3. Originating party abandons call. 4. A feature request is received from the originating party.
PIC7 Send Call	Authority of originating party to place call is verified.	SSP sends an indication of desire to set up a call to the specified Called Party ID to the terminating call portion.	1. Indication from terminating half BCM that the terminating party is being alerted. 2. Indication from terminating half BCM that the call cannot be presented to the terminating party (e.g., network congestion). 3. Indication from terminating half BCM that the terminating party is busy. 4. Indication from terminating half BCM that the call is accepted and answered by terminating party (e.g., terminating party goes off-hook). 5. Originating party abandons call. 6. A service/service feature request is received from the originating party.
PIC8 O_Alerting	Indication from terminating half BCM that the terminating party is being alerted of an incoming call.	SSP waits for the terminating party to answer.	1. Indication from terminating half BCM that the call is accepted and answered by terminating party (e.g., terminating party goes off-hook). 2. Indication from terminating half BCM that the terminating party does not answer within a specified time period. 3. Originating party abandons call. 4. A service/service feature request is received from the originating party.

(continued)

Table 6–1 *Continued*

Name	Entry Event(s)	Action(s)	Exit Event(s)
PIC9 O_Active	Indication from terminating half BCM that the call is accepted and answered by terminating party.	Connection established between calling and called party. Call supervision is provided.	1. A disconnect indication (e.g., on-hook) is received from the terminating party through the terminating half BCM. 2. A disconnect indication (e.g., on-hook) is received from the originating party. 3. A service/service feature request is received from the originating party.
PIC10 O_Disconnect	A disconnect indication is received from the originating party, or received from the terminating party via the terminating half BCM indicating timed release disconnect or release.	Connection is left intact and appropriate timing may be started depending on the indication received, the access type and the position of the SSP in the connection.	1. Completion of disconnection of call (e.g., expiration of disconnect timing, resource idled). 2. If terminating party goes off-hook before the timer expires, a called party reconnect event is sent to PIC 9. 3. A disconnect indication (e.g., on-hook) is received from the originating party. 4. A service/service feature request is received from the originating party.
PIC11 T_Null	Disconnect and clearing of previous call.	For a non-ISDN line, a conventional or SS7 trunk, or a private facility trunk, the line or trunk interface is idle (i.e., no calls exists), and the SSP provides supervision on the line or trunk. For an ISDN interface, although the call reference of the cleared call has been released, other calls may still exist.	Indication of incoming call received from originating half BCM.
PIC12 Authorize Termination	Indication of incoming call received from originating half BCM.	SSP verifies the authority to route this call to the terminating access (e.g., check business group restrictions, restricted incoming access to line etc.).	1. Authority to route call to specified terminating resource verified. 2. Authority to route call to specified terminating resource denied. 3. Indication of originating party abandon received from originating half BCM.

Name	Entry Event(s)	Action(s)	Exit Event(s)
PIC13 Select Facility	Authority to route call to specified termination resource verified.	The busy/idle status of the terminating access is determined.	1. Available terminating resource in resource group identified. 2. All resources in group busy or called party busy. 3. Indication of originating party abandon received from originating half BCM.
PIC14 Present Call	Available terminating resource identified.	The SSP informs the terminating access of the call (e.g., line seizure with power ringing, or Q.931 SETUP message).	1. Terminating party is alerted (e.g., power ring being applied). 2. Cannot present call (e.g., ISDN RELEASE message with busy cause). 3. Indication of originating party abandon received from originating half BCM. 4. Ringing timeout indication of called party no answer.
PIC15 T_Alerting	Terminating party alerted of incoming call.	SSP alerts the terminating resource and waits for the terminating party to answer.	1. Call is accepted and answered by terminating party. 2. Terminating party does not answer within a specified duration. 3. Indication of originating party abandon received from originating half BCM. 4. A service/service feature request is received from the terminating party.
PIC16 T_Active	An indication is sent to the originating half BCM that the terminating party has accepted and answered the call (e.g., terminating party goes off-hook).	Connection established between calling and called party. Call supervision is provided.	1. A disconnect indication (e.g., on-hook) is received from the terminating party. 2. A disconnect indication (e.g., on-hook) is received from the originating party. 3. A service/service feature request is received from the terminating party.
PIC17 T_Disconnect	A disconnect indication is received from the terminating party, or received from the originating party via the originating half BCM.	Connection is left intact and the appropriate timing may be started, depending on the access type and the position of the SSP in the connection.	1. Completion of disconnection of call. 2. Called party reconnected event. 3. A service/service feature request is received from the terminating party. 4. A disconnect indication (e.g., on-hook) is received from the originating party.

Table 6–2   TDPs

Originating TDP	Event	Message/Description
(e1) Origination Attempt	SSP considers an Origination Attempt event to have occurred when it receives an off-hook indication from an idle non-ISDN line, a SETUP message from an ISDN interface, an Initial Address Message (IAM) from an SS7 trunk or when a trunk within a Trunk Group (TG) supporting conventional signaling is seized, or a seizure signal is received on a private facility.	Origination_Attempt
(e2) Origination Attempt Authorized	SSP detects an originated event when the authority to place an outgoing call is verified.	Orig_Attempt_Auth SSP sends this message to the SCP/Adjunct at the Origination Attempt Authorized TDP when it detects an originated event that is reportable because it either satisfies a trigger criteria or was requested by an SCP/Adjunct.
(e3) Information Collected	SSP detects an information collected event when the complete initial information from the caller is available.	Info_Collected SSP sends this message to the SCP/Adjunct when an information collected event is detected and is reportable because it either satisfies a trigger criteria or was requested by an SCP/Adjunct.
(e4) Information Analyzed	SSP detects an information analyzed event when the CalledPartyID, the TypeOfCall, and when appropriate, the PrimaryTrunkGroup and PrimaryCarrierID parameters are determined by the SSP. The trigger analyses includes Carrier Identification Codes (CICs), 3/6 digits and 7/10 digit DN North American Numbering Plan (NANP) addresses, feature codes, carrier access codes, prefixes, customized dialing plan addresses.	Info_Analyzed SSP sends this message to the SCP/Adjunct when an information analyzed event is detected and is reportable because it either satisfies a trigger criteria or was requested by an SCP/Adjunct.
(e5) Route Selected	SSP detects a route selected event when the originating routing information for the call has been determined.	Route_Selected SSP sends this message to the SCP/Adjunct when it determines the routing of the call and the event is reportable because it either satisfies a trigger criteria or was requested by an SCP/Adjunct.

Originating TDP	Event	Message/Description
(e6) Origination Authorized	SSP detects an origination authorized event when the authority to place the call is verified. For an SS7 trunk interface, if the received IAM indicates that a continuity check is being performed on the call connection and the call terminates to an analog line or ISDN interface subtending the SSP, this event occurs when a continuity message (COT) with a successful indication is received from the originating access.	Origination_Authorized SSP sends this message to the SCP/Adjunct when it verifies the calling party's authorization to place the particular call and the event is reportable because it either satisfies a trigger criteria or was requested by an SCP/Adjunct.
(e7) O_Term. Seized	The SSP detects a O_Term. Seized event when an indication of a Call Accepted event is received from the terminating call portion or when certain abnormal cases occur in ISDN when the call is offered to an ISDN interface (or EKTS group) and no user equipment has responded.	O_Term_Seized SSP sends this message to the SCP/Adjunct when it receives indication from the terminating end that the call was delivered and the event is reportable because it either satisfies a trigger criteria or was requested by an SCP/Adjunct.
(e8) O_Answer	The SSP detects an O_Answer event when an indication of a connected event is received from the terminating call portion.	O_Answer SSP sends this message to the SCP/Adjunct when it receives an indication from the terminating end that the call has been answered and that a connection has taken place and the event is reportable because it either satisfies a trigger criteria or was requested by an SCP/Adjunct.
(e9) O_Abandon and O_Calling Party Disc.	SSP detects a O_Abandon and O_Calling Party Disc. event when the calling party disconnects, which can be the result of one of the following when a SSP receives: • An on-hook from a caller served by a non line (following flash timing), or • A call clearing message from a caller served by an ISDN interface, or • A disconnect indication for a conventional trunk or a private facility, or • A Release (REL) message fro an SS7 trunk.	O_Abandon_&_O_Calling_ Party_Disc The SSP sends these messages to the SCP/Adjunct if the near-end party goes on-hook and the event is reportable because it either satisfies a trigger criteria or was requested by an SCP/Adjunct.

(continued)

Table 6–2 *Continued*

Originating TDP	Event	Message/Description

(e10)
Feature Requested
	SSP detects a Feature Requested event from PICs 1, 3, 4, 5, and 6 when one of the following has occurred:
	• From an interface supporting ISDN Class I equipment, this corresponds to the ISDN user sending a feature activator. From PIC 1, is expected in an INFORMATION message with a null call reference value.
	    From PICs 3-6, this is expected in a SETUP or an INFOrmation message containing the call reference of the specific call.
	• This event is detected from PICs 3-6 when a switch-hook flash is entered from an analog line or private facility in the special situation where the user is initiating another two-party call in addition to an existing two-party call. Otherwise, this event cannot occur from a non-ISDN line, conventional or SS7 trunk, or from an interface supporting ISDN Class II equipment.
	    SSP detects Feature Requested events for Feature Requested triggers at the NULL, COLLECTING INFORMATION, ANALYZING INFORMATION, SELECTING ROUTE, AND AUTHORIZING CALL SETUP PICs.
		Feature_Requested
		SSP sends this message to the SCP/Adjunct when it detects that the user entered a feature activator and the event is reportable because it either satisfies a trigger criteria or was requested by an SCP/Adjunct.

(e11) O_Mid-Call	SSP detects a Feature Requested event when one of the following has occurred: • From a non-ISDN line or private facility, this event occurs when the user executes a switch-hook flash. • From an interface supporting ISDN Class I equipment, this corresponds to the ISDN user sending a feature activator, an ISDN HOLD message, or an ISDN RETRIEVE message. When the controlling leg applies to an EKTS group, a HOLD message can only be used to trigger AIN (or be treated as an event), when no other user in the EKTS group is connected to the call. If there are other users connected to the call, the HOLD message causes the user to be separated from the call, as defined under EKTS and is transparent to AIN. In addition, when the	Feature_Requested SSP sends this message to the SCP/Adjunct when it detects that the user depressed a flash-hook or a feature activator and the event is reportable because it either satisfies a trigger criteria or was requested by an SCP/Adjunct.

Originating TDP	Event	Message/Description
	controlling leg applies to an EKTS group, a RETRIEVE message can only be used to trigger AIN (or be treated as an event) if no user is connected to the call. If one or more users are already connected to the call, the RETRIEVE message causes the user to be connected to the call, as defined by EKTS, and is transparent to AIN. • This event cannot occur from a conventional or SS7 trunk, or from an interface supporting ISDN Class II equipment. SSP detects Feature Requested events for mid-call triggers at the CALL PROCEEDING, WAITING FOR ANSWER, ACTIVE, and RELEASE PENDING PICs.	
(e12) Cleared	SSP detects a Cleared event when an indication that the called party disconnected is received from the terminating call portion, which can result from the following: • For an intraswitch call to a non-ISDN line, the SSP receives an on-hook indication from the terminating line (and the SSP has provided switch-hook flash timing). • For an intraswitch call to an ISDN interface, the SSP receives a call clearing message from the terminating user. In addition, this occurs when a Call Rejected event is received from the terminating call portion that does not indicate that the user is busy. For an intraswitch call to an EKTS group, only one user in the terminating EKTS group is connected to the call and that user sends a call clearing message (if ISDN) or an on-hook indication (if an analog user, and switch-hook flash timing has been provided). Moreover, the Cleared event occurs when an EKTS user (in the terminating EKTS group) disconnects and under EKTS the switch determines that the call should be cleared. • For a conventional trunk or private facility, the SSP receives a disconnect signal. • For an SS7 trunk, a Release (REL) or a suspend (SUS) message is received.	O_No_Answer SSP sends this message to the SCP/Adjunct when the far party goes on hook and the event is reportable because it either satisfies a trigger criteria or was requested by an SCP/Adjunct.
(e13) O_Disc. Complete	SSP detects a O_Disc. Complete event that occurs when the timed release disconnect timer expires (at this SSP). For a terminating	O_Disc_Complete SSP sends this message to the SCP/Adjunct when it *(continued)*

Table 6–2   *Continued*

Originating TDP	Event	Message/Description
	access of an interface supporting ISDN Class I and Class II equipment, this event is equivalent to the O_Disconnect event.	determines that a O_Disc. Complete event has occurred and is reportable because it either satisfies a trigger criteria or was requested by an SCP/Adjunct.
(e14) Orig. Denied	SSP detects an Orig. Denied event when the authority to place an outgoing call is denied. This event does not apply for private facilities or an interface supporting ISDN Class II equipment. For conventional and SS7 TGs, this event occurs when glare is detected and the other call is given precedence.	Orig_Denied SSP sends this message to the SCP/Adjunct when it detects an Orig. Denied event that is reportable because it either satisfies a trigger criteria or was requested by an SCP/Adjunct.
(e15) Collect Timeout and Collect Information Failure	1. SSP detects a Collect Timeout event when complete initial information was not received before a normal interdigit timer expires. For an SS7 trunk the Collect Timeout event corresponds to the IAM not containing the information necessary to process the call. There is no timing involved. 2. SSP detects a Collect Information Failure event when it is unable to perform the information collection function because of a lack of switch resources (e.g., a digit collector is unavailable). This event can only be a requested event; it cannot be a trigger.	Collect_Timeout and Collect_Information_Failure SSP sends the first message to the SCP/Adjunct when a Collect Timeout event is detected that is reportable because it either satisfies a trigger criteria or was requested by an SCP/Adjunct. SSP sends the second message to the SCP/Adjunct when a Collect Information Failure event is detected that was requested by an SCP/Adjunct.
(e16) Invalid Info	SSP detects an Invalid Info event when the collected information is invalid	Invalid_Info SSP sends this message to the SCP/Adjunct when Invalid Info event occurs in the ANALYZING INFORMATION PIC and the event is reportable because it either satisfies a trigger criteria or was requested by an SCP/Adjunct.
(e17) Network Busy	SSP detects the Network Busy event when all the routes are busy.	Network_Busy SSP sends this message to the SCP/Adjunct when it determines that none of the

Originating TDP	Event	Message/Description
		routes identified during the SELECTING ROUTE PIC are available and the event is reportable because it either satisfies a trigger criteria or was requested by an SCP/Adjunct.
(e18) Auth. Failure	SSP detects the Auth. Failure event when the authority to place the call is denied. For an SS7 trunk interface, the Auth. Failure event occurs when a COT with a failure indication is received.	Auth_Failure SSP sends this message to the SCP/Adjunct when it determines that the calling party is not authorized to place a particular call because some restrictions apply and the event is reportable because it either satisfies a trigger criteria or was requested by an SCP/Adjunct.
(e19) O_Called Party Busy	SSP detects the O_Called Party Busy event indication when one of the following occurs: • An O_Called Party Busy event specifying user busy is received from the terminating portion of the call (i.e., network-determined-user busy or user-determined-user busy, or • A Presentation Failure event specifying user busy is received from the terminating call portion.	O_Called_Party_Busy SSP sends this message to the SCP/Adjunct when it is notified that a busy condition was detected at the terminating end and the event is reportable because it either satisfies a trigger criteria or was requested by an SCP/Adjunct.
(e20) Termination Attempt	SSP detects a Termination Attempt event when it receives an indication of a desire to deliver a call from the originating portion of the call.	Termination_Attempt SSP sends this message to an SCP/Adjunct when it detects a Termination Attempt event that is reportable because it either satisfies the trigger criteria or was requested by the SCP/Adjunct.
(e21) Term. Authorized	SSP detects a Term. Authorized event when the SSP determines that a call is authorized to be routed to a terminating user.	Term_Authorization SSP sends this message to an SCP/Adjunct when it detects a Term. Authorized event that is reportable because either satisfies the trigger criteria or was requested by the SCP/Adjunct.

(continued)

Table 6–2 *Continued*

Originating TDP	Event	Message/Description
(e22) Term. Resource Available	SSP detects a Term. Resource Available event when the SSP determines that an idle facility (e.g., a non-ISDN line, ISDN interface, trunk or private facility) or a position in a queue is available.	Term_ResourceAvailable SSP sends this message to an SCP/Adjunct when it detects a Term. Resource Available event that is reportable because it either satisfies the trigger criteria or was requested by the SCP/Adjunct.
(e23) T_Term. Seized	SSP detects a T_Term. Seized event when the called party is being alerted of the call. The Call Accepted event can be the result when the SSP: 1. Provides power ringing to the terminating non-ISDN line; or 2. Receives an ALERTING message or PROGRESS message from an ISDN user; or 3. Seizes a conventional trunk and no continuity check is required in the previous connection or, if a continuity check was required, a COT with a successful indication has been received; or 4. Receives an ACM for an SS7 trunk in response to an IAM; or 5. Seizes a private facility.	T_Term_Seized SSP sends this message to an SCP/Adjunct when it detects a T_Term. Seized event that is reportable because it either satisfies the trigger criteria or was requested by the SCP/Adjunct.
(e24) T_Answer	SSP detects a T_Answer event when the called party answers the call. A connected event can be the result when the SSP receives: 1. An indication that the terminating party served by an non-ISDN line when off-hook; or 2. A CONNect message from an ISDN user; or 3. An answer indication on a conventional trunk or private facility; or 4. An ANM for an SS7 trunk in response to an IAM.	T_Answer SSP sends this message to an SCP/Adjunct when it detects a T_Answer event that is reportable because it either satisfied the trigger criteria or was requested by the SCP/Adjunct.
(e25) T_Discon-nect	SSP considers a T_Disconnect event to be the result when the SSP: 1. Receives an on-hook indication from a non-ISDN line; or 2. Receives a call clearing message from an ISDN user (or a call terminating to an EKTS group, a user in the EKTS group has sent a	T_Disconnect SSP sends this message to the SCP/Adjunct when it detects a T_Disconnect event that is reportable because it either satisfies the trigger criteria or was requested

Originating TDP	Event	Message/Description
	call clearing message and under EKTS, the call is to be cleared); or 3. The SSP receives a disconnect signal from a conventional trunk or private facility; or 4. Receives RELEASE (REL) or SUSPEND (SUS) message for an SS7 trunk. 　　The T_Disconnect event may also result from error situations such as when an ISDN interface goes down (this may be detected at the data link layer of the protocol.	by the SCP/Adjunct.
(e26) T_Discon- nect Complete	SSP detects a T_Disconnect Complete event when the release timer expires (at this SSP). For a terminating access of an interface supporting ISDN Class I and Class II equipment, this event is equivalent to the Disconnected event.	T_Disconnect_Complete SSP sends this message to an SCP/Adjunct when it detects a T_Disconnect Complete event that is reportable because it either satisfies the trigger criteria or was requested by the SCP/Adjunct.
(e27) T_Mid-Call	SSP detects Feature Requested events for mid-call triggers at the ALERTING and ACTIVE PICs of the TBCM. The SSP detects a Feature Requested event when one of the following has occurred: 1. From the ALERTING PIC, the Feature Requested event corresponds to an ISDN Class I equipment user sending a feature activator. 2. From the ACTIVE PIC, the Feature Request corresponds to one of the following: 　• From a non-ISDN line or private facility, this event occurs when the user executes a switch-hook flash. 　• From a user served by ISDN Class I equipment, this corresponds to the ISDN user sending a feature activator, an ISDN HOLD message, or an ISDN RETRIEVE message. 　• This event cannot occur from a conventional or SS7 trunk, or from an interface supporting ISDN Class II equipment.	Feature_Requested SSP sends this message to an SCP/Adjunct when it detects a Feature Requested event that is reportable because it either satisfies the trigger criteria or was requested by the SCP/Adjunct.
(e28) T_Abandon & T_Calling Party Disc.	SSP detects a T_Abandon & T_Calling Party Disc. event when the terminating portion of the call receives indication that the originating portion is clearing.	T_Abandon_&_T_Calling_Party_Disc SSP sends these messages to an SCP/Adjunct when it

(continued)

Table 6–2   *Continued*

Originating TDP	Event	Message/Description
		detects a T_Abandon & T_Calling Party Disc. event that is reportable because it either satisfies the trigger criteria or was requested by the SCP/adjunct.
(e29) Term. Denied	SSP detects the Term. Denied event when the authority to route the call to the called party is denied.	Term_Denied SSP sends this message to an SCP/Adjunct when it detects a Term. Denied event that is reportable because it either satisfies the trigger criteria or was requested by the SCP/Adjunct.
(e30) T_Busy	SSP detects a T_Busy event when the terminating access is found to be busy. The T_Busy event may also be detected as a result of an analog line being out of order, marked as busy by a customer make-busy key, or as a result of certain maintenance actions.	T_Busy SSP sends this message to an SCP/Adjunct when it detects a T_Busy event that is reportable because it either satisfies the trigger criteria or was requested by the SCP/Adjunct.

(e31) Presentation Failure	SSP detects the Presentation Failure event when the call is rejected by the called party, or an expected response is not received for a call terminating to a trunk. A Presentation Failure event can be the result of one of the following occurring:
	1. A call cannot be rejected from a non-ISDN line.
	2. In ISDN (and EKTS), a call is rejected when one or more users send a call clearing message in response to the terminating call, or one or more users send any message other than an ALERTING or CONNECT message and call setup timers expire.
	3. For a conventional trunk or for a private facility, the call rejected event is detected when either of the following occur:
	  • The SSP does not receive the proper acknowledgment signals (e.g., an expected wink is not returned).
	  • The SSP receives a disconnect indication
		Presentation_Failure
		
		SSP sends this message to an SCP/Adjunct when it detects a Presentation Failure event that is reportable because it either satisfies the trigger criteria or was requested by the SCP/Adjunct.

Originating TDP	Event	Message/Description
	before an answer indication has been received. 4. For an SS7 trunk, the call rejected event is detected when any of the following occur: • The second attempt continuity check on the outgoing circuit fails. • The SSP receives a REL in response to an IAM. • The SSP does not receive a CRA after sending a CRM for the second time. • The SSP does not receive an ACM or ANM in response to the IAM in the allotted time (if timing is applied at the SSP). • The SSP receives a REL after an ACM has been received.	
(e32) T_No Answer	SSP detects the T_No Answer event when the called party does not answer before the switch-based ringing timer expires. This timer is used for services such as Call Forwarding on No Answer.	T_No_Answer SSP sends this message to an SCP/Adjunct when it detects a T_No Answer event that is reportable because it either satisfies the trigger criteria or was requested by the SCP/Adjunct.

In addition, AIN 0.2 has added procedures to align it with the ITU-T IN CS-1 release.

AIN 0.2 also provides additional features in relation to the intelligent peripheral (IP) interface. Most of these added features pertain to ISDN support. Moreover, callers now can interact with an IP directly or with a switch-based resource.

Several automatic message accounting (AMA) functions have been added to AIN 0.2, principally for more statistics on call durations and no responses.

Finally, the operations of AIN 0.1 have been enhanced in AIN 0.2, principally in memory administration, testing, traffic management, and data collection.

NEW CAPABILITIES IN GR-1298-CORE, ISSUE 3

The latest revision issued in 1996, is formally titled, "AIN Generic Requirements: Switching Systems" (AINGR). It is published in GR-1298-CORE, Issue 3, July 1996, Revision 1, November 1996. The remainder of this chapter examines this final revision.

Changes Made Between AIN 0.2 and the 1996 Revision

A few additions were in AIN 0.2 before the publication of the specification that is the main subject of the remainder of this chapter. A summary is provided here.

Service Data Function (SDF)

The SDF function was added to provide the ability for the SCP/adjunct to access data associated with a customers switch-based service such as call forwarding, selective call rejections, etc.

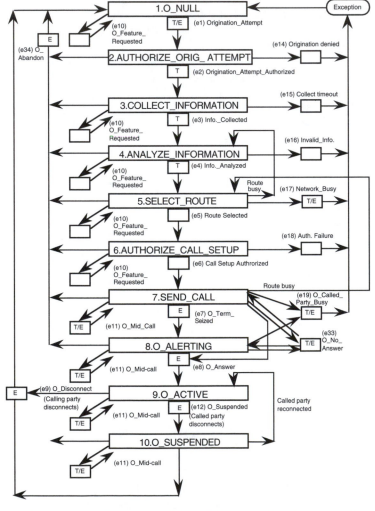

Figure 6–3   Bellcore AIN revision, origination model.

Create-Call Function

The SCP/adjunct is now able to request that a call be established on behalf of an end user by executing the create-call function. A new message, which is called the Create_Call message, is sent from the SCP/adjunct to the SSP.

Other Capabilities

The changes made between AIN 0.2 and the 1996 release also include additional AMA operations, enhanced call party handling, and remote access capabilities.

The Originating and Terminating BCM

Figures 6–3 and 6–4 show the revised originating and terminating BCM as published in AINGR. A comparision of Figures 6–1 and 6–2 will reveal that the two models are quite similar. However, AINGR has included many additional features and operations beyond AIN 0.1. AINGR is closely aligned with the ITU-T Capability Set 2 (CS-2), which has yet

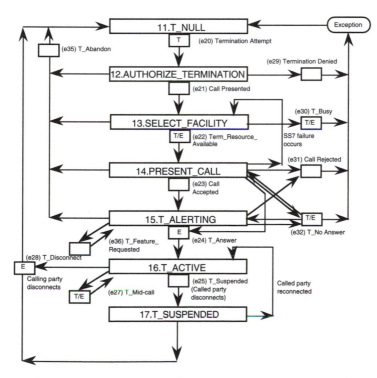

Figure 6–4   Bellcore AIN revision, termination model.

to see wide implementation. AINGR is a subset of CS-2, although AINGR has some capabilites not included in CS-2.

What Is Next?

Eventually, vendors will bring AINGR into their product-line, and operators will implement it as part of their network. Presently, AIN 0.1 is the mainstay for the Bellcore AIN. For the ITU-T, it is IN CS-1, the subject of the next chapter.

SUMMARY

The Bellcore AIN 0.1 defines the detailed operations of the advanced intelligent network. It is based on an originating basic call model (BCM) and a terminatng BCM. Both BCMs define the detection points, the triggers, and the points in call, as well as the messages that flow between the SSP and SCP, based in the rules defined in the BCMs.

7

A More Detailed Analysis
of the ITU-T IN Call Model
and Capability Set-1 (CS-1)

The focus of this chapter is on the ITU-T call model and CS-1. We begin the discussion with an examination of the basic call model (BCSM). A description of each PIC is provided (as we did in Chapter 6, with the Bellcore AIN model). In addition, examples are provided on how the BCSM is used in CS-1.

The next part of the chapter expands on the material in Chapter 3 dealing with the global functional plane (GFP), with the focus on service independent building blocks (SIBs). For this part, the reader should be familiar with the material pertaining to Figures 5–12 through 5–14 in Chapter 5.

The term "call party" is used in this chapter to connote either a calling or called party. Otherwise, the terms called party or calling party will be used in their proper context.

THE ITU-T BCSM

Figures 7–1 and 7–2 depict the ITU-T BCSM originating and terminating operations respectively. As noted earlier, this model is quite similar to its Bellcore counterpart, from the standpoint of PICs and DPs. Both models are based on the support of a conventional two-party call.

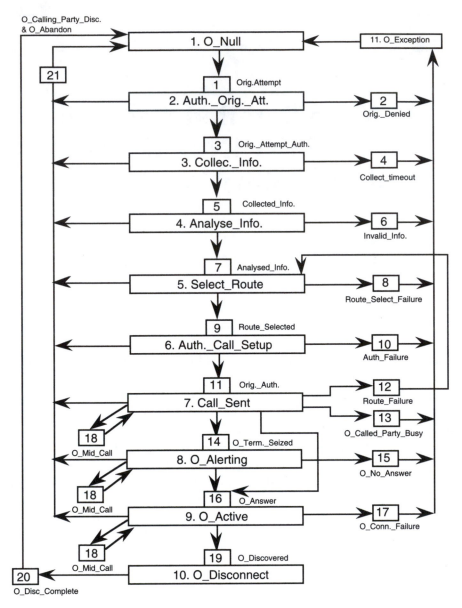

Figure 7–1   Originating BCSM.

Table 7–1 shows the major events that take place in the call model. As I did with the Bellcore model in Chapter 6, the entry events, actions, and exit events are described in text. You can refer to Figures 7–1 and 7–2 to correlate the text to the specific detection points.

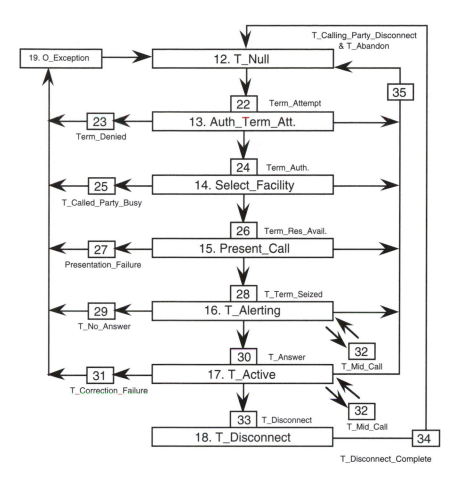

Figure 7–2   Terminating BCSM.

Table 7–1   PICs for ITU-T Call Model

Name	Entry Event(s)	Action(s)	Exit Event(s)
PIC1 0_Null	Disconnect and clearing of a previous call	Line or trunk interface is idle. Supervision is being provided.	Indication of desire to place outgoing call received from originating party. For example, a Q.931 SETUP message.
PIC2 Authorize_ Origination_ Attempt	Indication of desire to place outgoing call received from originating party.	Authority of user to place outgoing call with certain properties (e.g., line restrictions) is being verified.	1. Authority/ability to place outgoing call verified. 2. Authority/ability to place outgoing call denied.

(continued)

Table 7–1 *Continued*

Name	Entry Event(s)	Action(s)	Exit Event(s)
			3. Originating party abandons calls.
PIC3 Collect_ Information	Authority/ability to place outgoing call is verified.	SSP collects initial information (e.g., dialed address digits, service codes) from the user.	1. Availability of complete information from originating party. 2. Information collection error has occurred (e.g., invalid dial string format, digit collection timeout). 3. Originating party abandons call.
PIC4 Analyze_ Information	Availability of complete information from originating party	Information being analyzed according to the specified numbering plan. Routing address and type of calls (local, long distance) are determined.	1. Availability of routing address and call type. 2. Unable to analyze and translate dial string in the dialing plan. 3. Originating party abandons call.
PIC5 Select_ Route	1. Availability of routing address and call type. 2. Unable to complete call using specified route (e.g., congestion).	Routing address and call type interpreted.	1. Terminating resource to which call should be routed has been identified. 2. Unable to select a route (e.g., unable to find a correct route). 3. Originating party abandons call.
PIC6 Authorize_ Call_Setup	Terminating resource to which call should be routed is identified.	Authority of originating party to place call is verified.	1. Authority of originating party to place this call is verified. 2. Authority of originating party to place this call is denied. 3. Originating party abandons call.
PIC7 Call_Sent	Authority of originating party to place call is verified.	Call is processed by the terminating half BCSM, and originating BCSM awaits indication the call is presented to called party.	1. Indication from terminating half BCSM that the terminating party is being alerted. 2. Indication from terminating half BCSM that the call cannot be presented to the

Name	Entry Event(s)	Action(s)	Exit Event(s)
			terminating party (e.g., network congestion). 3. Indication from terminating half BCSM that the terminating party is busy. 4. Indication from terminating half BCSM that the call is accepted and answered by terminating party (e.g., terminating party goes off-hook). 5. Originating party abandons call. 6. A service/service feature request is received from the originating party.
PIC8 O_Alerting	Indication from terminating half BCSM that the terminating party is being alerted of an incoming call.	Waits for indication from terminating half BCSM that called party has answered; continue processing of call setup (ringing).	1. Indication from terminating half BCSM that the call is accepted and answered by terminating party (e.g., terminating party goes off-hook). 2. Indication from terminating half BCSM that the terminating party does not answer within a specified time period. 3. Originating party abandons call. 4. A service/service feature request is received from the originating party.
PIC9 O_Active	Indication from terminating half BCSM that the call is accepted and	Connection established between calling and called party. Call supervision is provided.	1. A disconnect indication (e.g., on-hook) is received from the terminating party through the terminating half BCM.

(continued)

Table 7–1 *Continued*

Name	Entry Event(s)	Action(s)	Exit Event(s)
	answered by terminating party.		2. A disconnect indication (e.g., on-hook) is received from the originating party. 3. A service/service feature request is received from the originating party. 4. A connection failure occurs
PIC10 O_ Disconnect	A disconnect indication is received from the originating party.	Disconnect treatment is applied.	1. Completion of disconnection of call (e.g., expiration of disconnect timing, resource idled).
PIC11 O_Exception	An exception is encountered.	Provide default handling of condition to ensure resources are not inappropriately allocated.	Default handling completed by SSF/CCF.
PIC12 T_Null	A disconnect and call clearing occurs.	Line/trunk is idled.	Indication of incoming call.
PIC13 Authorize_ Termination_ Attempt	Indication of incoming call received from originating half BCSM.	Authority to route this call to the terminating party is verified.	1. Authority to route call to specified terminating resource verified. 2. Authority to route call to specified terminating resource denied. 3. Indication of originating party abandon received from originating half BCSM.
PIC14 Select_ Facility	Authority to route call to specified termination resource group verified.	A resource in a specified resource group is being selected.	1. Available terminating resource in resource group identified. 2. All resources in group busy or called party busy. 3. Indication of originating party abandon received from originating half BCSM.
PIC15 Present_ Call	Available terminating resource identified.	Terminating resource is informed of incoming call (e.g., line seizure,	1. Terminating party is alerted (e.g., power ring being applied).

Name	Entry Event(s)	Action(s)	Exit Event(s)
	Q.931 SETUP message, SS7 ISUP IAM message).		2. Cannot present call (e.g., ISDN RELEASE message with busy cause). 3. Indication of originating party abandon received from originating half BCSM. 4. Ringing timeout indication of called party no answer.
PIC16 T_Alerting	Terminating party alerted of incoming call.	Indication sent to originating half of BCSM that terminating party is being alerted.	1. Call is accepted and answered by terminating party. 2. Terminating party does not answer within a specified duration. 3. Indication of originating party abandon received from originating half BCSM. 4. A service/service feature request is received from the terminating party.
PIC17 T_Active	An indication is sent to the originating half BCSM that the terminating party has accepted and answered the call (e.g., terminating party goes off-hook).	Connection established between calling and called party. Call supervision is provided.	1. A disconnect indication (e.g., on-hook) is received from the terminating party. 2. A disconnect indication (e.g., on-hook) is received from the originating party. 3. A service/service feature request is received from the terminating party. 4. A connection failure occurs.
PIC18 T_Discon-nect	A disconnect indication is received from the terminating party.	Disconnect treament is being applied.	1. Completion of disconnection of call.
PIC19 T_Exception	An exception condition is encountered.	Indication of condition is sent to originating half BCSM.	Default handling by SSF/CCF completed.

THE CALL MODEL IN CS-1

The BCSM is altered for CS-1. As before, there is an originating half BCSM and a terminating half BCSM, as shown in Figures 7–3 and 7–4. Both are managed by a separate BCM in the SSF/CCF.

Referring to Figure 7–3, which depicts the originating BCSM for CS-1, PIC 1 is the O_Null and Authorization_Origination_Attempt. The entry event for the PIC is a disconnect and the clearing of a previous call which could also be an abandon. The origination attempt, of course, depicts that a call is being attempted. During this operation, the SSF/CCF must have available considerable information that is associated with the originating call portion. Examples of this information (and not all inclusive) are as follows:

- Calling and called party numbers
- Bearer capability in accordance with Q.931 and Q.962
- Calling party business group ID (if appropriate)

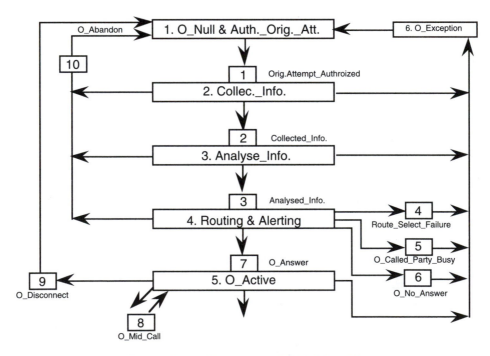

Figure 7–3   Originating BCSM for CS-1.

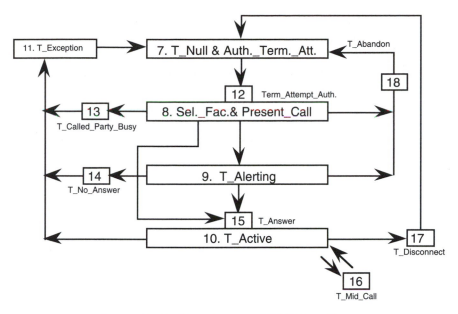

Figure 7–4   Terminating BCSM for CS-1.

- Feature code (which is defined in accordance with national standards)
- Operator services information
- Transit network selection (if appropriate)
- Other parameters pertaining to SS7 and ISDN operations

The exit event from this PIC is the indication that the outgoing call is permitted, which leads to the entry event into PIC 2 Collect_Information. If the reader has examined the previous material in this chapter, it should be evident that the CS-1 specification is simply a variation to the basic call model and this includes PIC 2 which consists of collecting information such as dial digits and service codes from the originating party. As with PIC 1, CS-1 requires that the SSF/CCF have sufficient information available to take further actions. The information cited in the previous list must be available as well as information dealing with the originating line, carrier access code/carrier identification code (e.g., 10XXX, etc.).

The exit event from PIC 2 is the availability of information from the originating party, which leads to the entry to the Analyze_Information PIC, which is PIC 3 in Figure 7–3. The function of this PIC is to analyze and translate information (specifically the dialed number) in accordance with the dialing plan to determine a routing address for the call. This PIC also determines the type of call such as a local exchange call, international call, a pay-phone call, etc.

The exit to PIC 3 is the availability of sufficient routing information to enter PIC 4, which is the routing and alerting operations (and actually encompasses four PICs of the basic BCSM: Select_Route, Authorize_Call_Setup, Call_Sent, and O_Alerting). The function of PIC 4 is to do route selection and to verify that the originating party is allowed to make this call through the route. This PIC is exited with: (a) an indication from the terminating half BCSM, (b) the call is answered by the called party, (c) by this party going off-hook or responding back with the proper Q.931 or ISUP message. The successful occurrence of these events will lead to the entering of the O_Active PIC which is numbered PIC 5 in Figure 7–3. The call remains in this PIC as long as the users are connected. The exit occurs with disconnect operations and other events such as a hook flash, an ISDN feature activator, etc.

The O-Exception PIC is just that, a PIC dealing with exception conditions such as errors in information flows to the SCF, and so on.

Figure 7–4 shows the terminating BCSM for CS-1. For PIC 7, the T-Null and Authorize_Termination_Attempt PICs are grouped together. The entry event to PIC 7 is a disconnect or clearing of a previous call or a number of exception conditions noted by SSF/CCF. The exit event from PIC 7 occurs with an indication of an incoming call from the originating half BCSM and the validation of the authority to route the call to a specified terminating party. The exit from PIC 7 leads to the entry to PIC 8, which consists of the Select_Facility and Present_Call PICS of the basic call model. The functions of PIC 8 consist of the determination that a particular resource is available and is being selected and the exit events consist of the terminating party being alerted.

These operations lead to the entry event into PIC 9, which is the T_Alerting PIC. As just mentioned, the entry event is the awareness that the called party is being alerted and the exit events consist of the call being accepted and answered by the called party. The exit from PIC 9 is the entry event to PIC 10, the T_Active PIC, which is executed during the ongoing call. PIC 10 is exited when disconnect operations occur and exception conditions occur (the latter shown in Figure 7–4) as PIC 11, T_Exception PIC.

So, this last analysis is actually somewhat redundant to the basic call model that was explained in the beginning of this chapter. Therefore, we expand this section and examine in more detail (a) the user operations in relation to this model, and (b) an examination of the actual interactions between the originate and terminate BCSMs. These two descriptions follow in the next two sections of the chapter, after which we examine the SIB architecture in more detail.

USER OPERATIONS IN RELATION TO THE BCSM

We now expand the analysis, and explain how the originating (calling) and terminating (called) users' operations relate to the BCSM. The examples assume the users are communicating with the network with an ISDN interface, and the Q.931 protocol. Appendix E provides a brief overview of the Q.931 messages used in the examples in this chapter.

In event 1, the user sends to the network the Q.931 SETUP message. In turn, the network responds with either a SETUP ACK or a RELEASE COMPLETE. The SETUP ACK acknowledges the user set up message, and if the connection cannot be made, the network sends the RELEASE COMPLETE message. These two options are shown as event 2 in Figure 7–5. In event 3, the user sends call information to the network in the INFORMATION message. At a minimum, the message must contain dialing information. As Figure 7–5 illustrates, the information gathering procedure is part of the Collec._Info. PIC. Next, the originating BCSM returns the CALL PROCEEDING message in event 4. This event occurs as part of the Analyse_Info. process.

The Routing and Alerting operations depicted in events 5, 6, and 7 entail the routing of the call to the called party in which the calling user is informed with the PROGRESS message (event 5). Once the called party is alerted, the network returns the ALERTING message to the calling user as depicted in event 6. If the called party is busy or does not answer, the calling user is notified with the RELEASE COMPLETE message shown as event 7. Event 7 may also entail the successful completion of the call in which the called party goes off hook. In this situation, event 7 is shown in the figure with the network sending a CONNET message to the calling party. In turn, this party returns the CONNECT ACK to the network, as shown in event 8. As Figure 7–5 illustrates, these operations are part of the BSCM O_Active process. Finally, the release operations occur in events 10 and 11 through the exchange of the RELEASE and RELEASE COMPLETE messages, respectively.

Figure 7–6 shows the operations at the terminating BCSM and the

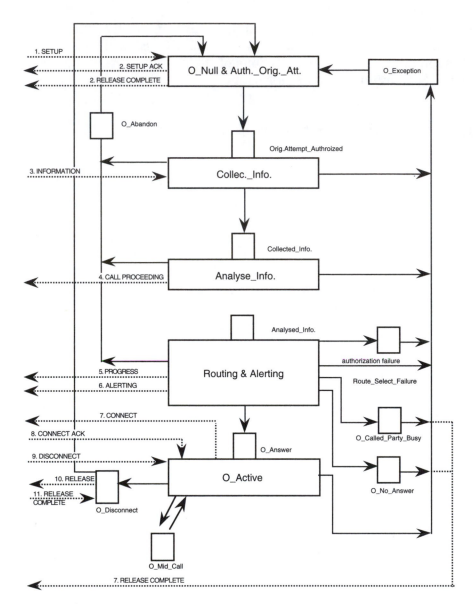

Figure 7–5   User interaction with originating BCSM.

context of how the BCSM interacts with the called party. Obviously, the operations for terminating a call for the T_BCSM occurs with the terminating PICs. The operations with the called party and the terminating BCSM mirror the operations between the calling party and the originating BCSM, as shown in events 1 through 10 in Figure 7–6.

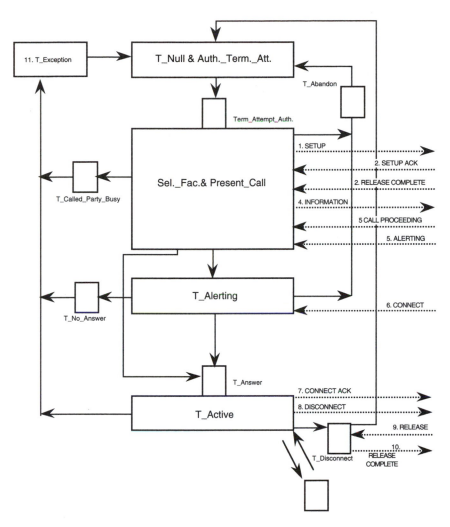

Figure 7–6   User interaction with terminating BCSM.

INTERACTIONS BETWEEN THE ORIGINATE AND TERMINATE BCSMS

Figure 7–7 shows the interactions that occur between the originate and terminate BCSMs, called the O-BCSM and T-BCSM respectively. The first interaction occurs when the calling party's call attempt is verified in PIC 4 of the O-BCSM. A message (an information flow) is sent to the T-BCSM, as shown in event 1. The interaction of the information flow is with PIC 7 in the T-BCSM.

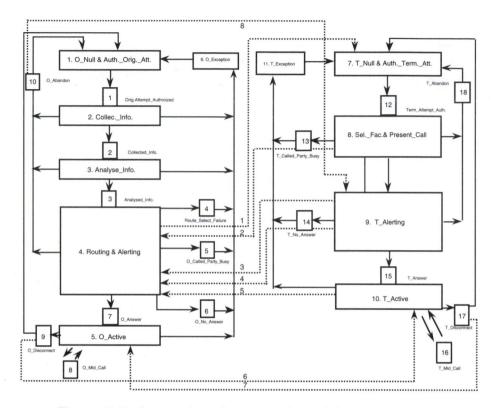

**Figure 7–7   Interactions between the originate and termi-
nate BCSMs.**

As a result of the interaction in event 1, the T-BCSM indicates to
the O-BCSM that the called party is busy (event 2), that the called party
is being alerted (event 3), or that the called party does not answer (event
4). In event 5, an indication is sent from the T-BCSM to the O-BCSM
pertaining information that the called party has answered the call. These
operations occur in PIC 10 at the T-BCSM and at PIC 4 at the O-BCSM.

In the situation when the calling party disconnects, an indication is
sent from the O-BCSM to the T-BCSM as shown in event 6. In turn, a disconnect from the called party is depicted in event 7. Finally, in event 8, the
O-BCSM informs the T-BCSM that the calling party has abandoned the call.

THE SERVICE INDEPENDENT BUILDING BLOCKS (SIBs)

We now move into a more detailed examination of the SIBs, which is
one of the key components in the IN. To begin this process, Figure 7–8

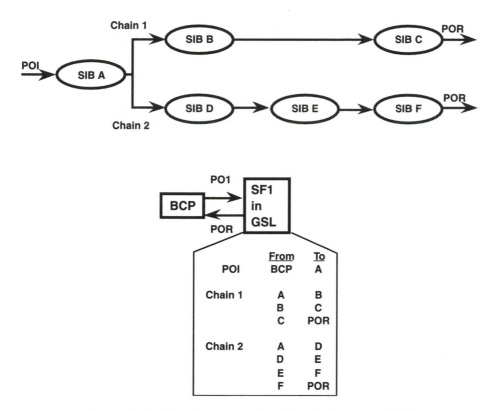

Figure 7–8   Service plane, functional plane, and SIBs.

shows another view of Figure 5–14 in Chapter 5. The IN service feature (SF) in the service plane is initiated by a trigger in BCP, and the chain of SIBs (which describes the SF) is obtained from the global service logic (GSL). New SFs SIBs are made available to the GSL.

In this example, the GSL describes SF1, which establishes the relationships of the SIBs. The POI instantiates SIB A, which leads to the execution of either chain 1 or chain 2, which then leads to the POR to the BCP.

SIB Functional Model and Functional Entities' Relationships

Figure 7–9 provides another view of the IN SIBs, their relationship to basic call processing, and to the functional entities. The numbers in the figure labeled r1 through r6 are reference to the interactions that occur between the functional entities. They are used to depict the information flows between the functional entities. Later examples in this chapter will make use of these reference points.

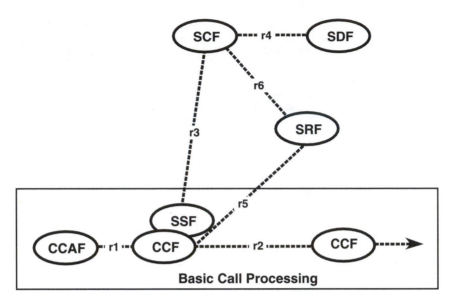

Figure 7–9 Functional model and functional entity relationships.

In addition, we need to iterate (from Chapter 5) how the SIBs (the functional entity operations) are numbered. Each is identified with a four-digit number XYYZ:

X   identifies the functional entity (2 represents the CCF/SSF, 3 represents the SRF, 4 represents the SDF, and 9 represents the SCF).

YY   identifies the SIB number

Z   distinguishes between functional entity actions that have a common XYY

Figure 5–13 in Chapter 5 is redrawn as Figure 7–10, and includes the reference points between the SRF, SCF, and CCF/SSF. We will use this example to explain the information flows beween the functional entities.

SIB Architecure

A standard method is used to describe the SIB operations, as depicted in Figure 7–11. The SIB has one logical start and one or more logical ends. The input and output to/from the SIB are two parameters: (a) call instance data (CID), and (b) service support data (SSD). Since the SIBs are service-independent (and independent from each other), these

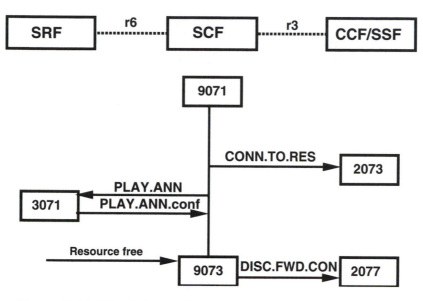

Figure 7–10   The information flows for the QUEUE SIB (and queue with announcement).

parameters have the effect of tailoring the SIB to a service feature. In effect, the generic SIB becomes service-dependent by coding different values into the CID and SSD parameters.

The connect to resource (CONN.TO.RES) information flow is an information flow that is executed by the SCF to request the CCF/SSF provide a connection toward an SRF. The intent is to provide a means to support user interaction. The information flows in the r3 reference. The play announcement (PLAY.ANN) information flow is used by the SCF to direct the SRF to apply a specific announcement toward the call party. The SCF sends back a confirm after the announcement has been played. The disconnect forward connection (DISC.FWD.CON) information flow is used by the SCF to direct the SCF to initiate a disconnection toward the user.

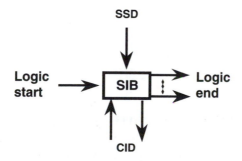

Figure 7–11   Representation of the SIB.

The specific operations of the functional entity actions (FEAs) are summarized as follows. Be aware that all these operations are defined in detail with SQL diagrams, and ASN.1 code, and Chapter 3 provides information on these tools.

Number	Actions
9071	Initiates the actions
	Stores a call reference for the operation
	Sets a timer for the operation
2073	SSF receives the connect to resource message
	Requests the CCF to connect the party to the appropriate SRF
3071	Plays the announcement as directed by the SCF
2077	Upon directed by the SCF, requests the CCF to disconnect the party from the SRF
9073	Dequeues call attempt based on availability of resource
	As directed, initiates disconnect
	Updates status of resource (busy, etc.)
	Returns control to SCF

Call Instance Data (CID)

The CID defines parameters that may change with each call instance, as examples, a PIN code, calling line ID, etc. Each CID value is associated with a logical name, called the CID field pointer (CIDFP). This field pointer identifies which CID is required by the SIB. If more than one CID is needed by the SIB, multiple field pointers can be used.

Service Support Data (SSD)

The SSD defines parameters that are specific to the SF description. GSL specifies the SSD values for the SIB. The SSD is coded with: (a) fixed parameters, which are not determined by the call instance, but by the service/SF description, and (b) field pointers, which identify which CID is needed by the SIB (these pointers are CID FPs, described earlier).

EXAMPLE OF AN IN OPERATION WITH SIB INVOCATIONS

This part of the analysis will piece together several of the concepts covered in this and earlier chapters. The BCP example in Chapter 5 (see

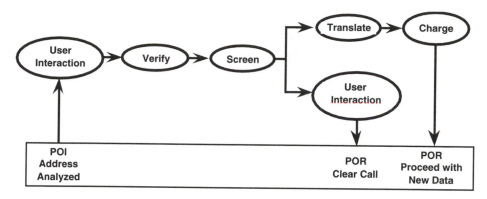

Figure 7-12 Global service logic (GSL) for SIB operations example.

Figure 5-14) will be expanded and explained in more detail. Figure 5-14 is redrawn here as Figure 7-12 to aid the reader during this discussion.

Basic Call Process (BCP) SIB

The BCP SIB is redrawn yet again as Figure 7-13 in accordance with the conventional SIB representation we introduced in Figure 7-8. Recall from discussions in earlier chapters, that the BCP is a specialized SIB that is used to provide basic call processing and acts as the point of initiation (POI) to the execution of other SIBs and the point of return (POR) from these SIBs. Consequently, the output of the BCP SIB serves as input to the other SIBs, and the output of the last executed SIB serves as input to the BCP SIB.

The service support data is output from the BCP and contains a set of POIs which specify the points in the BCP where the IN processing can occur for a specific service. The service support data also contains six CIDFPs whose functions are as follows[1]:

---

[1]The reader should be aware that the ITU-T Q.1213 specification contains an inconsistency in describing the BCP SIB, in that it cites the use of the CIDFP-Call reference field pointer but does not show it in the diagram in the document (which is Figure 18 of Q.1213). Moreover, Figure 18 shows a CIDFP-Error field pointer but does not describe its use in the specification. I have notified ITU-T of this inconsistency. It seems logical to conclude that the figure as drawn in this book as Figure 7-12 is correct since I see no reason why the BCP SIB would convey error values to the other SIBs. Indeed, error detection should be handled by the BCP initially and other errors detected by the other SIBs should then be passed back to the BCP at the POR. I have shown the BCP SIB as it is illustrated in Q.1213.

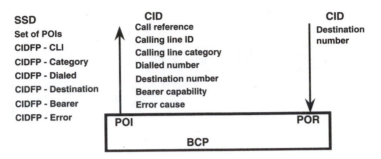

Figure 7–13 Basic call process (BCP) SIB.

- CIDFP-CLI (calling line ID): Specifies which call instance data is to be used as the calling line identifier
- CIDFP-Category: Specifies which call instance data is to be used as the CLI category data
- CIDFP-Dialed: Specifies which call instance data is to be used as the dialed number
- CIDFP-Destination: Specifies which call instance data is to be used as the destination number
- CIDFP-Call reference: Specifies which call instance data is to be used to identify the call reference
- CIDFP-Bearer: Specifies which call instance data is to be used as the calling line identification bearer capability

The BCP also outputs call instance data consisting of the following information:

- Calling line identity: Specifies the network address from which the call originated
- Calling line category: Specifies the characteristics of the calling line such as an operator-indicated call, a call emanating from a pay telephone
- Dial number: Specifies the digits dialed by the caller
- Destination number: Also specifies the number dialed by the caller but this number is different from the dial number in that it has been modified through IN service processing
- Call reference: Identifies the specific call
- Bearer capabilities: Specifies the ISDN bearer capabilities that are being requested by the user (as examples, request for circuit or

packet mode services, identification of callers encoding and compression algorithm [A-law, μ-law], request for rate adaptation [as an example, adapting a data rate from 19.2 kbit/s to 64 kbit/s]).

The logical input to the BCP occurs at the POR and depends on the output of the last executed SIB.

USER INTERACTION SIB

The USER INTERACTION SIB allows information to be exchanged between the network and a calling or called party (see Figure 7–14). This SIB collects information from a call party and provides information to the party, for example in the form of announcements. The information provided by the network can take the form of audio messages, DTMF tones, and network progress signals such as dial tones or busy tones. The collected information can be DTMF tones, audio from the user, or strings of text.

The service support data consists of five sets of values shown in Figure 7–14, which are summarized here. The announcement parameters specify which announcement is to be sent to the user and, if the announcement is repeated, which parameters are used to stipulate the number of times the announcement will be repeated and the delay (in seconds) between repetitions.

The collect info parameters stipulate the information that is to be gathered from the user. These parameters stipulate the type of user information that is expected, such as audio, DTMF, or text string. The parameters also provide information that determines if an announcement

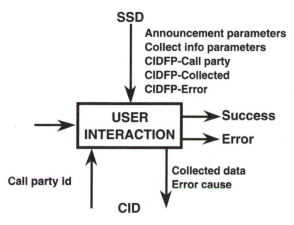

Figure 7–14   USER INTERACTION SIB.

can be interrupted by the call party entering information. Information is also provided specifying the maximum or minimum characters to collect, the time-to-wait for the beginning of the call party's response, the time-to-wait after a pause from a call party, and the method used to determine the end of the call party's input.

The CIDFP-Call party is a field pointer specifying which call instance data is to be used to identify the call party. The CIDFP-Collected field pointer specifies the location of the call party enter data. Finally, the CIDFP-Error field pointer specifies where the error causes will be written.

The call instance data contains the Call Party ID, which specifies the data that is associated with the CIDFP-Call party. The CID output Collected data specifies the data that is Collected from the call party and the Error cause identifies an error that occurred during the operation of this MIB (as examples, no input received during a timing period, call is abandoned, incorrect number of digits received, etc.).

The logical end to the USER INTERACTION SIB is success or error, which are used to determine if the user interaction occurs successfully or unsuccessfully.

VERIFY SIB

The VERIFY SIB is essentially an edit function (see Figure 7–15). Its purpose is to verify that the information received is consistent with what is expected. As a general practice, the information obtained from the USER INTERACTION SIB is verified. It follows then, that the VERIFY SIB is usually executed after the USER INTERACTION SIB is executed.

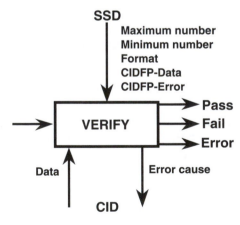

Figure 7–15   VERIFY SIB.

The service support data contains the maximum and minimum number of characters allowed as well as the expected syntax of the verified data. Therefore, the input stream is edited against the format values.

The CIDFP-Data is a field pointer specifying which call instance data is to be verified. The CIDFP-Error field pointer specifies where the error cause will be written.

The logical end of the VERIFY SIB is pass, fail, or error, which specify the results of the verification process. The CID output is an error cause which identifies an error that occurred during the operation of the CID.

SCREEN SIB

The SCREEN SIB is used to examine an identifier to determine if it is present in a list identified in SIB support data (see Figure 7–16). A match condition occurs if the identifier is found in the list. Examples of using the SCREEN SIB would be to verify a password, such as a PIN or a caller ID. The SIB is also used for originating call screening, account card calling, credit card validation, terminating call screening, and security screening.

The service support data contains the screen list name, which simply identifies the screen data object that is to be used. The screen list filter identifies the attributes and tests that are to be applied to the screen data object. The CIDFP-Authorized relationship ID is a field pointer that specifies which data is to be used for the relationship ID. In turn, this ID provides the identity of an pre-established IN authorized relationship.

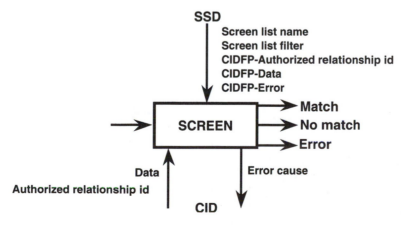

Figure 7–16   SCREEN SIB.

The CIDFP-Data filed pointer specifies which data is to be used as the identifier. The CIDFP-Error field pointer specifies where the error cause will be written. The CID contains the data value which is the attribute values associated with the CIDFP-Data, and it also contains the authorized relationship ID.

The logical end to the SCREEN SIB is either a match on the list, a no match on the list, or an error during the operation of this SIB. The CID output is an error cause which identifies an error that occurred during the operation of the CID.

TRANSLATE SIB

As the name TRANSLATE SIB implies, this part of the IN system provides a translation process on input information (see Figure 7–17). The output is the results of the translation. Examples of the TRANSLATE SIB are (a) translating DTMF tones to an E.164 address, (b) translating abbreviated dialing digits to a full address, (c) translating user-specific routing to network-specific routing, etc.

The service support data contains the object name, which stipulates where the data is located; the translate filter, which identifies attributes and filter tests to be applied to the data; and the translated attribute, which specifies the translated objects that are returned to the translated data values.

The service support data contains four CIDFPs. The CIDFP-Filter value(s) is a field pointer or pointers which specifies which data is to be

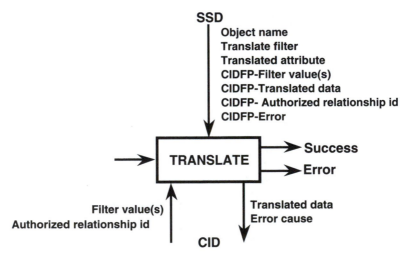

Figure 7–17   TRANSLATE SIB.

used as information; the CIDFP-Translated data, which is a field pointer which specifies where in the call instance data the translated data attributed value is to be written; the CIDFP-Authorized relationship ID, which was discussed earlier, and the CIDFP-Error field pointer, which was also discussed earlier. The input call instance data contains the filter values which specify the translate filter data values that are to be used in the operation and the authorized relationship ID.

The logical end to the TRANSLATE SIB is success or error and the output call instance data is the translated data (the result of the operation) and an error cause (if necessary).

CHARGE SIB

The CHARGE SIB is used for charging for the use of IN resources and is used to identify (a) the resources that are to be charges, and (b) where the charges are to be directed (see Figure 7–18). However, this SIB is not responsible for the conventional subscriber billing process, but the goal is to make the output of this SIB compatible with the overall charging and billing system of the service provider. Examples of typical resources applicable to the charge SIB are: SRF resources, such as voice messaging storage; packet transmission services; and overall bearer services.

The service support data includes the number of accounts that are to be charged, including an account identifier as well as the resource type that is to be charged. The units parameter specifies the type of value that

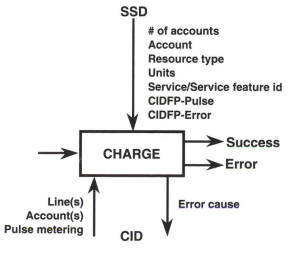

Figure 7–18   CHARGE SIB.

is associated with the charge. The service/service feature ID identifies the support service for which charging is applied. Two CIDFPs are employed with the CHARGE SIB. The CIDFP-Pulse field pointer specifies which data are to be used to identify pulse metering on the calling line. The CIDFP-Error field pointer, as before, specifies where the error cause will be written.

The input call instance data contains a line (s) value which is used to specify the line or lines for charging as well as an account number or number(s) for charging. The pulse metering parameter indicates that pulse metering is associated with the calling line.

The output to the CHARGE SIB is success or error and the output CID is the error cause (as examples, invalid account, invalid service feature, invalid resource, invalid units, etc.).

INFORMATION ON THE OTHER SIBs

As I stated in the introductory part of this chapter, the previous section has been used to show an example of an IN service. Consequently, this chapter does not cover in detail all the SIBs in the ITU-T IN specification. For the reader who wishes more information on the other SIBs in the model as well as more detailed aspects on how they are employed should refer to ITU-T Recommendation Q.1213.

SUMMARY

The ITU-T IN Model is a detailed and extensive specification on how to design and program the intelligent network modules. The IN design team can make use of SIB descriptions, the basic model, SQL, and ASN.1, all of which are spelled-out in several hundred pages of a well-designed and well-thought-out standard. Capability Set 1 (CS-1) is the prevalent standard now being used in the industry. It is expected that CS-2 will appear in products in 1998 or 1999.

8

Tools for the IN: X.700 and CMIP

This chapter provides an overview of the ITU-T network management specification, published in the X.700 Recommendations. The emphasis is on the X.700 and X.711 Recommendations, known as the Common Management Information Service Element (CMISE) and Common and Common Management Information Protocol (CMIP), respectively.

ROLE OF X.700 AND CMIP IN IN OPERATIONS

Several references have been made to the role of X.700 and CMIP in the operations of the IN. In Chapter 3, I emphasized that X.700 and CMIP, as network management tools, enhance the IN operations. Notwithstanding, X.700 and CMIP are not required for the IN to operate, but they are part of the total picture and are viewed as key components in the IN picture for the future, the subject of Chapter 10. So, to complete this picture and as a prelude to Chapter 10, let us take a look at X.700 and CMIP. As we proceed through this chapter, it will become evident that CORBA and TMN (Chapter 4) are associated with many of the X.700 and CMIP concepts.

LAYER ARCHITECTURE OF OSI MANAGEMENT

The OSI Model forms the underlying structure for the X.700 and CMIP standards, as well as the IN standards. An application entity is involved in OSI management. It is called the *systems management application entity (SMAE)*. It is responsible for implementing the OSI system management activities. An SMAE is a collection of cooperating application service elements (ASEs).

The OSI management model is consistent with the overall OSI application layer architecture. One configuration is shown in Figure 8–1. Other configurations are permissible.

The systems management application service element (SMASE) creates and uses the protocol data units (PDUs) transferred between the management processes of the two machines. These data units are called

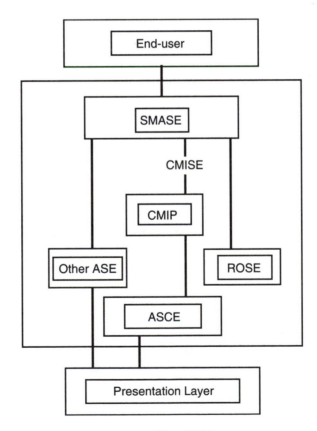

Figure 8–1   The OSI layers.

management application protocol data units (MAPDUs) and are examined later in the book.

The SMASE may use the communications services of application services elements or the common management information service element (CMISE). As shown in the figure, the use of CMISE implies the use of ROSE and ACSE.

In accordance with OSI conventions, two management applications in two open systems exchange management information after they have established an application context. The application context uses a name that identifies the service elements needed to support the association. The application context for OSI management associations implies the use of Association Control Service Element (ACSE), Remote Operations Service Element (ROSE), CMISE, and or more SMASEs.

STRUCTURE OF THE OSI MANAGEMENT STANDARDS

Table 8–1 lists the OSI management standards. This section provides an overview of each.

Management Framework

The foundation OSI management specification is X.700. It provides the concepts and definitions for OSI management. It also introduces the five major functional components of OSI management: accounting, security, configuration, fault, and performance. In addition, it explains the concepts of individual layer management and the concepts of managed objects.

Systems Management Overview

X.701 identifies the underlying OSI services used by the management entities. It describes the concepts of distributed systems management, introducing the agent and management processes. X.701 also establishes the structure for the applications layer interactions among the ASEs.

OSI MANAGEMENT FUNCTIONAL AREAS

For purposes of organization and documentation, five OSI management functional areas have been defined by the ITU-T and ISO. Be aware that these areas are actually contained in the separate documents

Table 8–1   The X.700 Series Recommendation Standards

Title	ITU-T
Management Framework	X.700
Systems Management Overview	
Structure of Management Information	
Management Information Model	X.720
Definition of Management Information (10165-2)	X.721
Guidelines for Definition of Managed Objects (10165-4)	X.722
Common Management Information Service Element (CMISE)	X.710
Common Management Information Protocol (CMIP)	X.711
Systems Management-Configuration Management	X.730
Object Management	X.730
State Management	X.731
Relationship Management	X.732
Systems Management-Fault Management	
Alarm Reporting	X.733
Event Reporting Management	X.734
Log Control Function	X.735
Confidence and Diagnostic Test Classes	X.737
Systems Management-Security Management	
Security Alarm Reporting Function	X.736
Security Audit Trail Function	X.740
Objects and Attributes for Access Control	X.741
Systems Management-Accounting Management	
Accounting Metering Function	X.742
Systems Management-Performance Management	
Workload Monitoring Function	X.739
Measurement Summarization Function	X.738

listed in Table 8–1 and the reader should study these documents for more information on the functional areas.

The functional areas are:

- Fault management
- Accounting management
- Configuration management
- Security management
- Performance management

Fault Management

Fault Management is used to detect, isolate, and repair problems. It encompasses activities such as the ability to trace faults through the system, to carry out diagnostics, and to act upon the detection of errors in order to correct the faults. It is also concerned with the use and management of error logs.

Accounting Management

This function is needed in any type of shared resource environment. It defines how the usage, charges, and costs are to be identified in the OSI environment. It allows users and managers to place limits on usage and allows for the negotiation of additional resources. As of this writing, this functional area is not well defined, and it will probably be some time before the standard is approved as an international standard. However, the document contains enough detailed information for planning purposes.

Configuration Management

This facility is used to identify and control managed objects. It defines the procedures for initializing, operating, and closing down the managed objects and the procedures for reconfiguring the managed objects. It is also used to associate names with managed objects and to set up parameters for the objects. Lastly, it collects data about the operations in the open system in order to recognize a change in the state of the system.

Security Management

This facility is concerned with protecting the managed objects. It provides the rules for authentication procedures, the maintenance of access control routines, the supporting of the management of keys for encipherment, the maintenance of authorization facilities, and the maintenance of security logs. It is in the formative stages, but it is certain that it will rely extensively on the directory service standards (X.500) for security support.

Performance Management

Performance management supports the gathering of statistical data and applies the data to various analysis routines to measure the performance of the system.

It permits the use of models to determine (1) if a system is meeting the required throughput, (2) if a system is providing adequate response time, (3) if a system is approaching overload, and (4) if a system is being used efficiently.

The performance management facility relies on many definitions and concepts that have been developed for the other layers of OSI, such as residual error rate, transit delay, connection establishment delay, and so on. Many of these definitions are widely used in X.25 and connectionless networks. In addition, this standard provides directions on how to apply sampling formula to the analysis. At the broadest level, performance management is organized around monitoring, analysis, and tuning functions.

COMMON MANAGEMENT INFORMATION SERVICE ELEMENT (CMISE)

CMISE is defined in X.710. As the title suggests, it identifies the service elements used in management operations as well as their arguments (parameters). It also provides a framework for common management procedures that can be invoked from remote locations.

CMISE is organized around the following types of services:

- M-EVENT-REPORT: This service is used to report an event to a service user. Because the operations of network entities are a function of the specifications of the managed objects, this event is not defined by the standard but can be any event about a managed object that the CMISE user chooses to report. The service provides the time of the occurrence of the event as well as the current time.

- M-GET: This service is used by CMISE to retrieve information from its peer. The service uses information about the managed object to obtain and return a set of attribute identifiers and values of the managed object or a selection of managed objects. It can only be used in a confirmed mode, and a reply is expected.

- M-CANCEL-GET: This service is invoked by the CMISE user to request a peer to cancel a previously requested M-GET service. It can only be used in a confirmed mode, and a reply is expected.

- M-SET: A CMISE user can use this service to request the modification of attribute values (the properties) of a managed object. It can be requested in a confirmed or nonconfirmed mode. If confirmed, a reply is expected.

- M-ACTION: This service is used by the user to request that another user perform some type of action on a managed object. It can be requested in a confirmed or nonconfirmed mode. If confirmed, a reply is expected.
- M-CREATE: This service is used to create a representation of another instance of a managed object, along with its associated management information values. It can only be used in a confirmed mode and a reply is expected.
- M-DELETE: This service performs the reverse operation of the M-CREATE. It deletes an instance of a managed object. It can only be used in a confirmed mode, and a reply is expected.

COMMON MANAGEMENT INFORMATION PROTOCOL (CMIP)

X.711 establishes the protocol specification for CMIP. CMIP supports the services listed in Table 8–2. These services were explained in the previous section. Notice that some of the services are confirmed, nonconfirmed, or have an option of using either the confirmed or nonconfirmed operation. These services allow two OSI management service users to set up actions to be performed on managed objects, to change attributes of the objects, and to report the status of the managed objects.

Like the other OSI protocols, CMIP must follow rules on the composition and exchange of PDUs. All the CMIP PDUs are defined by ASN.1. The operations are defined in ROSE with the OPERATION and ERROR external macros. Because of its dependence on ROSE, CMIP does not contain state tables, event lists, predicates, or action tables. Figure 8–2 shows these relationships in more detail.

Table 8–2   CMIP Services

Service	Type of Confirmation
M-EVENT-REPORT	Confirmed/nonconfirmed
M-GET	Confirmed
M-SET	Confirmed/nonconfirmed
M-ACTION	Confirmed/nonconfirmed
M-CREATE	Confirmed
M-DELETE	Confirmed

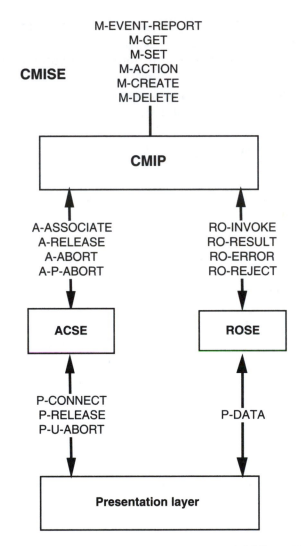

Figure 8–2   CMISE service elements with ACSE and ROSE.

The CMISE user, which is an SMASE of the OSI Model, issues and receives M-EVENT reports, M-GETs, M-SETs, M-ACTIONs, M-CREATEs, and M-DELETEs. CMIP acts upon these service definitions by invoking the primitives to ROSE. ROSE in turn uses the PDATA primitive to convey information back and forth between the presentation layer.

For the creation of the application association, CMIP, an SMASE, or a user application must avail itself of the services of ACSE through the A-ASSOCIATE, A-RELEASE, or A-ASSOCIATE service definition.

Earlier releases of CMISE/CMIP provided for the M-INITIALIZE, M-TERMINATE, and M-ABORT services. These were deleted from later releases of the standards. It is left to the user to determine how to establish the application association through ACSE.

Notwithstanding, ISO 9595 does define the parameters that are to be passed with A-ASSOCIATE service in order to establish a peer-to-peer application association. It must be the first instance of any OSI network management activity.

THE CMIP SCOPING AND FILTERING OPERATIONS

The term *scoping* can be used in conjunction with the containment tree and filters. Scoping describes the selection of a set of the managed objects in the management information tree (MIT) to which a filter is to be applied (see Figure 8–3).

Scoping works as follows. OSI network management permits the definition of levels of managed objects. Again, this is implemented in the form of a hierarchy as discussed earlier. The base object is the higher level identifier in the identification tree. The scoping permits a managing process to specify the level of detail in the accessing of the objects in the tree. Remember that this tree is defined as a containment tree. Therefore, identifiers are passed that allow the protocols to describe the level that is affected by the operation. It might be base object only, it might be the entire MIT, or it might be down to an nth level.

As part of this process it may be necessary that the return of information about the scoping operation requires multiple reporting transactions. Consequently, the scoping effect might also require multiple replies. These replies are called *linked replies*. They allow an agent process to report on actions or events on all or selected objects within the base object tree, without continuous queries from the managing process.

CMIP/CMISE can implement *filtering* operations to determine which events in a network are to be acted upon or reported. Filters are defined with ASN.1 to contain a set of assertions about the presence of attributes or the values of attributes in a managed object. If the filter operation is to test more than one assertion, the Boolean operators **and, or,** and **not** can be employed to group the assertions together. The network management protocols use a distinguished name with a filter to identify the managed object. An attribute can be evaluated by an equality assertion, a greater-than-or-equal-to assertion, a less-than-or-equal-to assertion, or a substrings assertion.

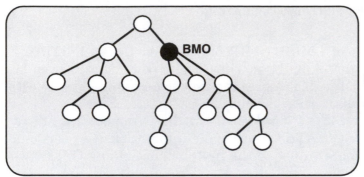

(a) BMO alone.

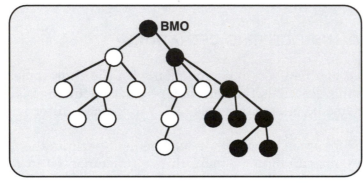

(b) BMO
& all MOs
in subtree
below BMO.

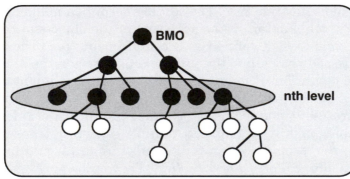

(c) BMO
& all MOs
to a specified
nth level
below BMO.

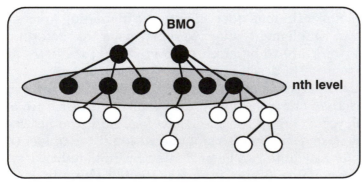

(d) All MOs
below BMO
to a specified
nth level.

Figure 8–3   Scoping.

CMISFilter is a CHOICE type that allows choosing a filter item or any of the three Boolean operators. In turn, FilterItem is also a CHOICE type, which allows choosing one of five types for matching: (1) equality, (2) a substring of objects, bits, etc., (3) greater than or equal to, (4) less than or equal to, or (5) the presence of a value.

RELATIONSHIPS OF CMISE AND CMIP

Figure 8–4 shows the relationships of CMISE and CMIP at a local site and a remote site. It depicts how the CMISE primitives are used to create CMIP protocol data units and how the CMISE parameters are

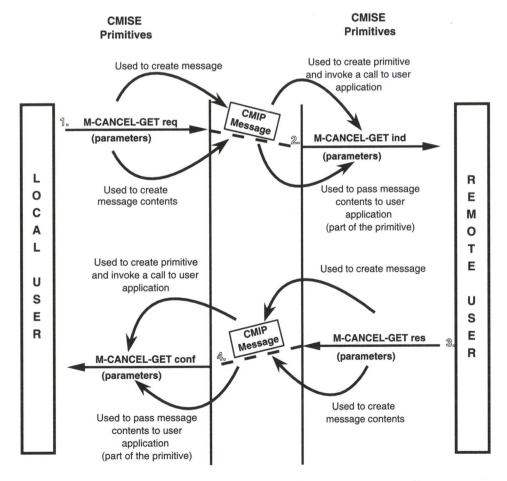

Figure 8–4   CMIP and CMISE operations.

used to determine the contents of the fields of the CMIP protocol data unit.

SUMMARY

The ITU-T X.700 Recommendations are a supporting part of the intelligent network. Strictly speaking, X.700 is not required for an IN operations, but is viewed as a support tool for the IN nodes.

9

ServiceBuilder

A wide variety of AIN/IN commercial products are now available in the marketplace. This chapter describes one such product developed by Nortel, called ServiceBuilder. This system is developed to provide rapid deployment of services with products based on the international standards from ITU-T and Bellcore. The ServiceBuilder adheres to Capability Set 1/Refined (CS-1/R). It also operates with IS-41 and SS7 (see Figure 9–1). In addition, ServiceBuilder will evolve to the support of Bellcore's AIN 0.2 Call Model.

SERVICEBUILDER CONFIGURATION

ServiceBuilder provides IN services such as number translation, virtual private networks (VPNs), and locations of personal communications services (POS) users. It also supports an array of credit card services, including the automated calling card services (ACCS) as well as prepaid phone calls. Figure 9–2 shows the ServiceBuilder architecture.

ServiceBuilder's architecture is organized around SIB libraries consisting of C++ code and application programming interfaces (APIs). The interactions of the SIBs are governed by the service logic execution envi-

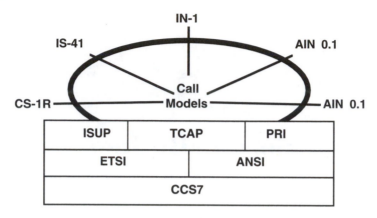

Figure 9–1   ServiceBuilder architecture.

ronment (SLEE). This entity allows the service provider to tailor services in a more flexible manner than traditional service creation operations.

Upon receiving an SSP query, the message is decoded and the subscriber records are retrieved as well as modules from the SIB library. A combination of this information and the service logic interpreter enable ServiceBuilder to provide the response from the SCP.

In the spirit of the IN concept, the SIBs are "plug and play." Some new services can be created by placing the SIBs in different order. Of

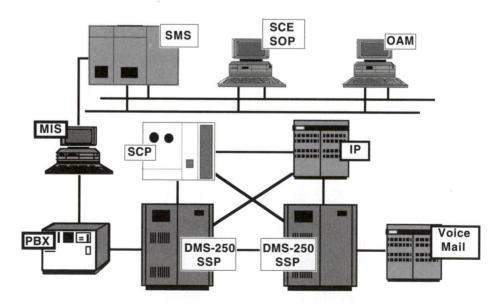

Figure 9–2   ServiceBuilder configuration.

course, if a SIB is not available to fulfill a service, a new SIB is created with the intent of making it generic enough to be used again.

As Figure 9–3 illustrates, the SEPs are duplexed as are the databases at the SEPs. Likewise, the SMSs consist of dual servers with one server active and the other server operating in warm standby. In addition, the SMS server disk subsystem uses disk mirroring to ensure the integrity of the database. The system is designed to where a single point-of-failure will result with no data loss.

Because market needs vary, the SCP is available in multiple configurations: One is based on commercial computer platforms and the other on a scalable Nortel DMS platform. The following two options are available to network providers:

- Computer-based ServiceBuilder SCP provides a system initially based on a Hewlett-Packard platform and open to other vendor designs. This configuration supports operations and maintenance capabilities, an SS7 front end, a relational database management system, as well as a software utilities for monitoring services and recording billing data.

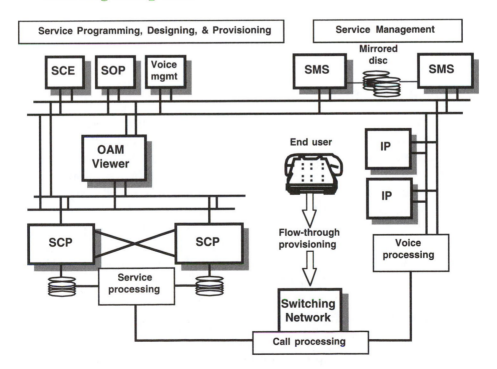

Figure 9–3   System architecture.

- DMS-based ServiceBuilder SCP uses SS7 protocol management software and DMS OAM&P facilities with interfaces to current operations support systems.

ServiceBuilder IP

The ServiceBuilder IP capabilities translate into a variety of applications for both local and toll carrier markets, including:

- Record, play and replay announcements of customer audio menu applications
- Dual-tone multifrequency digit collection for caller validation and access
- Customer routing profiles and routing override for "follow-me" services
- Call origination, bridging, and termination for "meet-me" or "page-me" services
- Digit and/or voice authentication for subscriber toll call validation service
- Data storing and forwarding for fax transfer services
- Interactive text-based dialog using the analog display services interface protocol for special transaction-based services

ServiceBuilder SMA

The ServiceBuilder SMS and SCE use a common client-server system architecture and a common server. The system is built on Hewlett-Packard servers and workstations, with the client stations supporting all human interactions with the system. The SMS supports various applications that collect data from network SCPs, ensure SCP software and data integrity, monitor service transactions, and manage the release of subscriber record and service profile updates to SCPs. SMS provisioning screens, created via the SCE, can be partially data filled creating "templates." These templates can be viewed, copied, added, deleted, and modified to speed the service order process.

ServiceBuilder SCE

The ServiceBuilder SCE is designed for quick service development, customization, and release to market. Services can be newly created or refashioned to meet special needs or customer requirements.

The SCE provides a network simulator to verify new and modified services prior to live network deployment. Modular, reusable IN software components (Service-independent Building Blocks, or SIBs) avoid any need for UNIX or C++ programming experience and are the principal tools for developing multiple services across all ServiceBuilder platforms—and other IN-compliant platforms, as well. SIBs are grouped into libraries for uniform manipulation by IN designers, network provider personnel, or third-party software developers.

Once a service has been defined (by graphically manipulating SIB icons on a screen), it can be simulated in a virtual network environment (also graphically defined) to show its operation at every stage. The service provisioner can use the SCE to graphically design the service order templates that will be used by the order entry clerks. The complete service definition (execution logic and provisioning screens) is then downloaded to the SMS.

AIN/IN SERVICES

This section describes some of the AIN/IN services provided by ServiceBuilder.

500 Service

With the 500 service, subscribers can customize a service to meet their needs. The service will map the 500 number to one terminating line at a time (according to time-of-day and other user-defined instructions). More advanced implementations will have the number ringing multiple lines in sequence to "find" the subscriber. To make changes, the subscriber dials into his or her personal file, which indicates where calls should be routed according to time of day, day of week, or special customer profiles.

Additional features of 500 service are:

- *Call screening:* Allows the subscribers to define who can reach them and when, according to Calling Line ID or PIN code.
- *Time dependent routing:* The network routes the incoming calls to different phones depending on time of day/day of week that calls are made.
- *Billing options:* For regular 500 service, the caller will pay for any toll charges. However, the subscriber can specify that if the call

originates from certain numbers (e.g., children at college), or if the caller enters a PIN, then the subscriber pays for the call.

- *Voice mail:* The subscriber can define a voice mail number so that under predefined circumstances, the call is routed to the subscriber's voice mail.

Fraud Control

Telephone fraud losses in the United States now exceed $3 billion each year—more than those of automatic teller machines and the major credit cards combined.

Long distance card fraud is a major contributor to these losses, from "shoulder surfers" who loiter near public phone booths to bogus security representatives "validating" card numbers by phone.

ServiceBuilder protects a user from calling card fraud losses with a variety of capabilities that can be tailored to the unique requirements of the user network. With the following options, an office alarm, account lockout, and/or follow-up report is triggered to thwart the fraud attempts.

Multiple Card Fraud Control—Usage Characteristics

- *PIN hunting:* Presets a threshold for invalid Personal Identification Number (PIN) attempts.
- *Card hunting:* Presets a threshold for card validation failures to the same PIN.
- *Compromise/threshold:* Creates a threshold for the total number of calls made on any one card for a set time period.
- *Geographic dispersion:* Flags physical separation between successive calls that is not consistent with single or multiple users. For example, a single user card account number used on the east coast is then used on the west coast 30 minutes later.
- *Concurrent calling:* Identifies calls originating from geographically separate locations made at the same time.

Single Card Fraud Control—On a Per-call Basis

- *Credit limits:* Reports an abnormally high call charge, based on usage characteristics of a preset threshold.
- *Call duration:* Flags calls that exceed a preset call-duration threshold.

- *Inactive account:* Identifies an attempt to access an inactive account.

Other Fraud Control—Working with End User

- Restricting billing types from specified originating numbers.
- Blocking card access to calling regions/countries where calls are not authorized.
- Setting thresholds for the number of validation queries within specified time increments.
- Capturing information on invalid queries.
- Generating reports for informed fraud investigation.

Follow Me

As a personal 800 service for individual subscribers, "follow me" connects callers with the ambulatory subscriber, with an 1-800 number.

Here's how it works:

- Each user is identified by Personal Call Manager software—a personal agent.
- To make changes, the subscriber calls into his or her "temporary time window," which indicates where calls should be routed for a specific time of day, day of week, or perhaps a holiday period.
- Calls can be screened by indicating numbers that are not to be forwarded.
- Security codes restrict access to the subscriber's call routing profile.

Time-Dependent Routing

Time-dependent routing is offered for 800 subscribers who wish to extend business hours, reduce toll charges, and improve customer service. The subscriber specifies a time-of-day, day-of-week, holiday, day-of-cycle, or a custom time window for which incoming calls are to be routed to a specific location.

Emergency Routing

Emergency routing allows all 800 calls to be diverted to a backup location, without customers even knowing there was a problem.

Outgoing Call Management (OCM)

With OCM, the subscriber preselects just what type of calls can be placed from his or her telephone. Unwanted 900 calls, long distance calls, directory assistance, and so on can all be restricted. Subscribers may customize the OCM service based on their own needs. The call restriction can also apply to certain telephone numbers or designated area codes. Moreover, the subscriber can override all restrictions personally by typing in a PIN code before placing the call.

OCM has obvious applications to telephones in public areas such as lobbies and waiting rooms. But it can also be applied (with time-of-day scheduling) to whole offices of telephones that are unattended at night and on weekends. Long distance bills can finally be brought under tight control.

Parents will appreciate the ability to restrict certain calls when children are learning to use the telephone. Roommates sharing a phone can use multiple PIN numbers, allowing each person to associate his or her long distance calling with an individual PIN, all of which is reflected on the monthly bill.

SUMMARY

This chapter highlighted an actual AIN/IN product, Nortel's ServiceBuilder. Other hardware and software vendors offer systems similar to ServiceBuilder.

10

Vision for the Future

This chapter examines how the intelligent network will play a role in future telecommunications systems. The future vision is based on research currently being conducted in Europe.

CONVERGENCE OF TECHNOLOGIES

Figure 10–1 shows the development of technologies and systems that have contributed to IN since 1985, and the prediction of where they will be at the turn of this century. By 2000 it is envisioned that many systems will migrate to third-generation mobile systems (TGMS). This figure is a creation of British Telecom, several standards groups, and amplified with some authors' views.

Paging has been implemented in different countries by a variety of systems. One of the more popular networks is called POCSAG (Post Office Code Standardization Advisory Group). It is a third-generation system and is employed in several countries in Europe. It operates in the 150 MHz to 170 MHz frequency band (depending on the country). The pan-European digital paging system is called ERMES, which stands for European Radio Message System. This technology is supported throughout the European Community (EC).

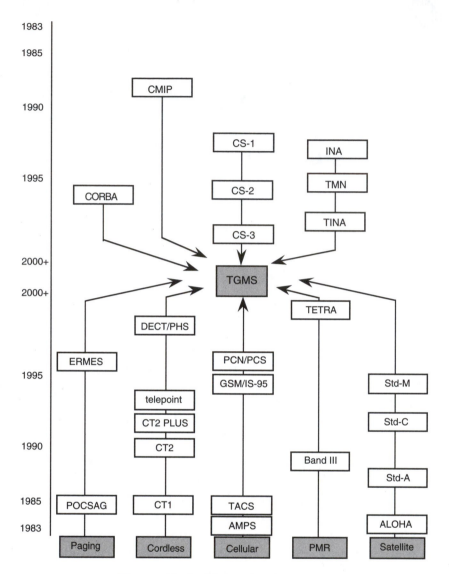

Figure 10–1   Vision for the future.

Cordless telephony (CT) has enjoyed some success in various parts of the world. Initially this technology was intended for private wireless PBX applications. It led to the development of the telepoint technology, which was targeted for the mass market. Telepoint has not been very successful because it relied on an existing population of CT2 handsets and CT2 has not been very successful, and interest was beginning to surface in higher frequency digital services.

The DECT technology evolved about the same time as CT2. It was originally called Digital European Cordless Telephony and is now renamed Digitally Enhanced Cordless Telephony. Its principal goal is to support a high-density subscriber population typically found in offices and campuses and to support higher bit rates for data applications. It also operates over the 1880 to 1900 MHz band.

Cellular telephony was introduced worldwide in the early 1980s (for example, 1983 in the United States, 1985 in the United Kingdom). The U.S. deployment was with the Advanced Mobile Phone System (AMPS). The U.K. system is based on AMPS and is called TACS (Total Access Communications System). These analog-based systems operate in the 900 MHz range and are known as first-generation mobile wireless systems.

The second-generation mobile wireless systems are known as either personal communications network (PCN) or personal communications services (PCS). These systems are based on the Global System for Mobile Technology (GSM) and the IS-95 standard. Unlike AMPS and TACS, these systems are digital and operate in the 1800 MHz to 1900 MHz bands. However, a number of systems are in operation that use GSM or IS-95 on the conventional 900 MHz band.

Private mobile radio networks (PMRs), as the name implies, are not part of a national pubic communications network, although they are regulated by the respective telecommunications administrations within each country. Initially, PMR systems were analog-based but they are evolving to the digital technology with the adoption of a European wide standard called TETRA (TransEuropean Trunked Radio).

Finally, mobile satellite systems are seen as both a complement to the systems just described or in some cases as a competitor. Considerable interest has focused recently in what are called satellite PCN (Personal Communications Networks) or satellite PCS (Personal Communications Services). Their unique attribute is their low-earth orbits (LEOs), which require the deployment of many satellites to cover the earth, yet allow the use of relatively inexpensive low-power mobile handsets. They also employ elaborate switching techniques in the satellites to support a user connection end-to-end, without the need to transport the signals on any terrestrial switching points until the signal reaches the called party.

The vision for the third-generation mobile system is the convergence of the somewhat disparate technologies into a common interworking architecture. This architecture is forecasted by network planners to provide broadband services, bandwidth-on-demand, multimedia services, and asymmetrical bandwidth. In other words, it is designed to provide the same type of user services as its wire-based counterpart known as broadband ISDN (B-ISDN) or simply broadband networks.

The top part of the figure shows the role that network management and intelligent networks are playing and will be playing in TGMS. The common management information protocol (CMIP) was the first worldwide effort in developing a standardized network management platform. CORBA (Common Object Request Broker Architecture) was developed in the late 1980s and implemented in the 1990s to provide a procedure for defining how objects interact in a distributed environment. Well-known object request brokers are used in many object-oriented network management systems.

Bellcore has provided extensive research leading to the information network and architecture (INA) that led to the subsequent development of the telecommunications management network (TMN) published in the ITU-T M.3010. These specifications have provided a worldwide framework for developing a unified network management system, which in turn has contributed to the telecommunications networking architecture (TNA).

UMTS AND FPLMTS AND THE IN SCF AND SDF

The concepts discussed in this chapter are also referred to as the universal mobile telecommunciations system (UMTS) in Europe. The ITU-T uses the term future public land mobile telecommunications system (FPLMTS).

While many details are still to be worked out, most agree that the IN SCF will be used to receive a mobile call (a so-called UMTS terminal), and initiate location operations by assessing an IN SDF for the location of the UMTS terminal and related information, such as call profiles. In effect, the SCF and SDF perform the functions of today's home/visitor location registers.

The focus of this book has been on intelligent networks with the emphasis on the work done by Bellcore and ITU-T. The evolution of the worldwide standards have taken place through capability sets. It is anticipated that in the future, capability set 3 (CS-3) will provide the final glue (of course, with revisions throughout) to the ITU-T view of the intelligent networks. As Figure 10–1 suggests, it is anticipated (and being planned by the Europeans) that these technologies will eventually converge into the TGMS.

Appendix A

OSI Basics

PROTOCOLS AND LAYERS

Machines communicate through established conventions called protocols. Since computer systems provide many functions to users, more than one protocol is required to support these functions. A convention is also needed to define how the different protocols of the systems interact with each other to support the end user. This convention is referred to by several names: network architecture, communications architecture, or computer-communications architecture. Whatever the term used, most systems are implemented with layered protocols.

In the OSI Model, a layer is considered to be a service provider to the layer above it (see Figure A–1). This upper layer is considered to be a service user to its lower layer. The service user avails itself of the services of the service provider by sending a transaction to the provider. This transaction informs the provider as to the nature of the service that is to be provided (at least, requested).

Insofar as possible, the service provider does provide the service. It may also send a transaction to its user to inform it about what is going on.

At the other machine (B in this figure), the operation at A may manifest itself by the remote service provider accepting the traffic from service provider A, providing some type of service, and informing the remote user about the operation. This user may be allowed to send a transaction back to its provider, which may then forward traffic back to A. In turn, service provider A may send a transaction to user A about the nature of

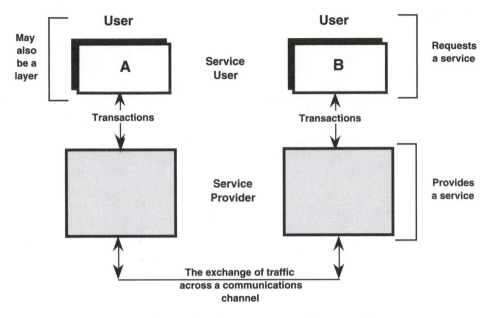

Figure A–1   The layer as a service provider.

the remote operation. The OSI Model provides several variations of this general scenario.

The end user rests on top (figuratively speaking) of the application layer (see Figure A–2). Therefore, the user obtains all the services of the seven layers of the OSI Model.

In accordance with the rules of the model, a layer cannot be bypassed. Even if an end user does not wish to use the services of a particular layer, the user must still "pass through" the layer on the way to the next adjacent layer. This pass-through may only entail the invocation of a small set of code, but it still translates to overhead.

However, every function in each layer need not be invoked. A minimum subset of functions may be all that is necessary to "conform" to the standard.

DESIGN PRINCIPLES

The OSI Model uses several principles to determine the number and nature of the OSI layers (see Table A–1). A close examination of these principles reveals that they closely follow the design principles of structured techniques and atomic actions and many of the IN concepts described in the main body of this book. The idea of these principles is to keep the software (and hardware) as modular and as simple as possible. The principles apply to (1) layers, (2) sublayers, and (3) entities within layers and sublayers.

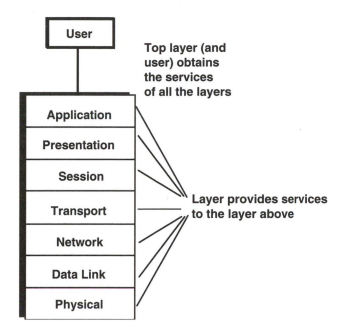

Figure A–2   Services of the full OSI Model.

Table A–1   Design Principles for the OSI Layers

P1   For simplicity, keep the number of layers within a small limit.

P2   Create layer boundaries that minimize layer interactions and the description of services.

P3   Separate layers should exist in which functions are different from each other.

P4   Similarly, place similar functions in the same layer.

P5   Select layer boundaries that past experience shows have functioned successfully.

P6   As a complement to P4, localized functions should be established that allow a redesign with minimal effect to adjacent layers.

P7   Create boundaries that might permit the corresponding interface to be standardized.

P8   As a complement to P4, create a layer when the data must be handled differently.

P9   As a complement to P6, changes made in a layer should not affect other layers.

P10 Each layer has boundaries (interfaces) only to its upper and lower adjacent layers.

For the use of sublayers, similar principles apply:

P11 As a complement to P3, P4, P6, P8, P9, and P10, create further subgrouping, if necessary.

P12 Create sublayers to allow interface with adjacent layers.

P13 Sublayers may be bypassed if the services are not needed.

Appendix B

SS7 Support of the Intelligent Network

SS7 FUNCTIONS

Intelligent networks that are defined in the ITU-T and Bellcore standards require the use of the Signaling System Number 7 (SS7) services. Therefore, it will be helpful for you to read this material if you are not familiar with SS7.

SS7 defines the procedures for the setup and clearing of a call between telephone users. It performs these functions by exchanging control messages between the SS7 components that support the end users' connection.

The SS7 signaling data link is a full duplex, digital transmission channel operating at 64 kbit/s. The SS7 link operates on both terrestrial and satellite links. The actual digital signals on the link are derived from pulse code modulation multiplexing equipment or from equipment that employs a frame structure. The link must be dedicated to SS7. In accordance with the idea of clear channel signaling, no other transmission can be transferred with these signaling messages and extraneous equipment must be disabled or removed from an SS7 link.

Figure B–1 depicts a typical SS7 topology. The subscriber lines are connected to the SS7 network through the service switching points (SSPs). The SSPs receive the signals from the customer and perform call processing on behalf of the user. SSPs are implemented at end offices or access tandem devices. They serve as the source and destination for SS7

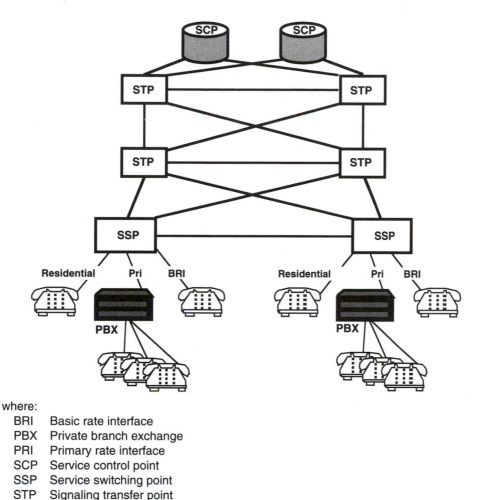

where:
   BRI   Basic rate interface
   PBX   Private branch exchange
   PRI   Primary rate interface
   SCP   Service control point
   SSP   Service switching point
   STP   Signaling transfer point

Figure B–1   Typical SS7 topology.

messages. In so doing, SSP initiates SS7 messages either to another SSP or to a signaling transfer point (STP).

The STP is tasked with the translation of the SS7 messages and the routing of those messages between network nodes and databases. The STPs are switches that relay messages between SSPs, STPs, and service control points (SCPs). Their principal functions are similar to the layer 3 operations of the OSI Model.

The SCPs contain software and databases for the management of the call. For example, 800 services and routing are provided by the SCP.

They receive traffic (typically requests for information) from SSPs via STPs and return responses (via STPs) based on the query.

Although Figure B–1 shows the SS7 components as discrete entities, they are often implemented in an integrated fashion by a vendor's equipment. For example, a central office can be configured with an SSP, an STP, an SCP, or any combination of these elements.

The SSP

The service switching point (SSP) is the local exchange to the subscriber and the interface to the telephone network. It can be configured as a voice switch, an SS7 switch, or a computer connected to switch.

The SSP creates SS7 signal units at the sending SSP and translates them at the receiving SSP. Therefore, it converts voice signaling into the SS7 signal units, and vice versa. It also supports database access queries for 800/900 numbers.

The SSP uses the dialed telephone numbers to access a routing table to determine a final exchange and the outgoing trunk to reach this exchange. The SS7 connection request message is then sent to the final exchange. In an IN, the SSP is responsible for receiving a customer's call and creating an IN message to send to the STP and/or SCP.

The STP

The signal transfer point (STP) is a router for the SS7 network. It relays messages through the network but it does not originate them. It is usually an adjunct to a voice switch and does not usually stand alone as a separate machine.

The STP is installed as a national STP, an international STP, or a gateway STP. Even though SS7 is an international standard, countries may vary in how some of the features and options are implemented. The STP provides the conversions of the messages that flow between dissimilar systems. For example, in the United States the STP provides conversions between ANSI SS7 and ITU-T SS7.

STPs also offer screening services, such as security checks on incoming and/or outgoing messages. The STP can also screen messages to make certain they are acceptable (conformant) to the specific network.

Other STP functions include the acquisition and storage of traffic and usage statistics for OAM and billing. If necessary, the STP provides an originating SSP with the address of the destination SCP.

The SCP

The service control point (SCP) acts as the interface into the telephone company databases. These databases contain information on the subscriber, 800/900 numbers, calling cards, fraud data, and so on. The SCP is usually linked to computer/databases through X.25. The SCP address is a point code, and the address of the database is a subsystem number (addresses are explained shortly).

Bellcore provides guidance on SCP databases, but BOCs vary in how they use them. The most common databases used are:

- Business Services Database (BSDB)
- Call Management Service Database (CMSDB)
- Line Information Database (LIDB)
- Home Location Register (HLR)
- Visitor Location Register (VLR)

In the IN, the SCP contains the IN data and IN processing modules.

The SS7 Levels (Layers)

Figure B–2 provides a view of the SS7 levels (layers). MTP level 1 performs the functions of a traditional OSI physical layer. It generates and receives the signals on the physical channel.

MTP level 2 relates closely to the OSI layer 2. It is a conventional data link level, and is responsible for the delivery of traffic on each link between SS7 nodes. The traffic in the upper layers of SS7 are encapsulated into MTP 2 "signal units" (this term is used instead of the conventional HDLC "frame") and sent on to the channel to the receiving node. This node checks for errors that may have occurred during transmission and takes remedial action (discussed later).

MTP level 3 performs OSI layer 3 functions, notably, the routing of messages between machine and between components within a machine. It performs load sharing operations across multiple links and reconfiguration operations in the event of node or link failure.

SCCP corresponds to several of the operations associated with OSI layer 3 (and although not generally discussed in literature, OSI layer 4, as well). Some of its principal jobs are: (1) supporting the MTP levels with global addressing, (2) providing connectionless or connection-oriented services, and (3) providing sequencing and flow-control operations.

The transaction capabilities application part (TCAP) corresponds to several of the functions of the OSI layer 7. It uses the remote operations

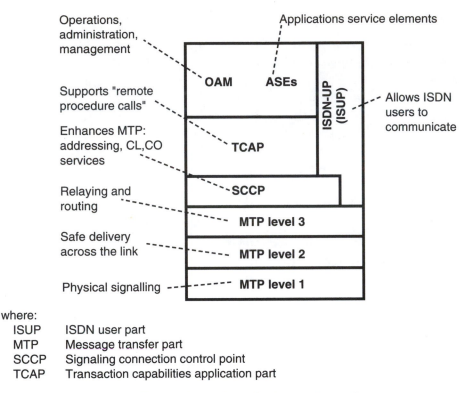

Figure B–2 illustration labels:

Operations, administration, management

Applications service elements

Supports "remote procedure calls"

Enhances MTP: addressing, CL,CO services

Relaying and routing

Safe delivery across the link

Physical signalling

OAM   ASEs

ISDN-UP (ISUP)

Allows ISDN users to communicate

TCAP

SCCP

MTP level 3

MTP level 2

MTP level 1

where:
  ISUP   ISDN user part
  MTP   Message transfer part
  SCCP   Signaling connection control point
  TCAP   Transaction capabilities application part

Figure B–2   The SS7 levels (layers).

service element (ROSE). As such, it performs connectionless, remote procedure calls on behalf of an "application" running on top of it.

Finally, the ISDN user part (ISDN-UP or ISUP) provides the services needed to support applications running in an ISDN environment.

An MTP 3 routing label is coded in every SS7 message and consists of the three fields shown in Figure B–3: the signaling link selector (SLS), the origination point code (OPC), and the destination point code (DPC). The OPC and DPC have been discussed previously. The SLS is used to select the signaling link within a given link set. The OPC and DPC are the addresses used in SS7 to route traffic between nodes. These addresses are used in an intelligent network when the IN SSP must form an IN query to the IN STP or IN SCP. The point codes are used to route the IN query and response to the proper IN nodes.

SCCP ADDRESS TRANSLATION

One of the more important tasks of SCCP is the addressing and address translation services performed for the user layers and MTP 3.

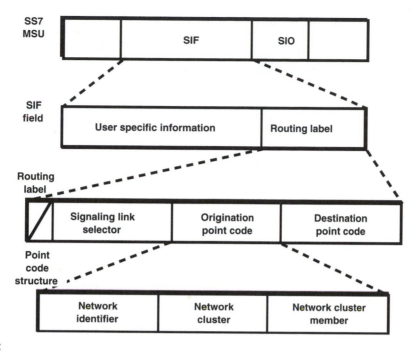

where:
SIF   Signalling information field
SIO   Status indicator octet

Figure B–3   Routing label.

Table B–1 shows the calling/called addresses and other identifiers that can be carried in the SCCP messages.

Most of these fields have been explained in previous parts of this book, but a brief word about the SSN should be helpful. The subsystem number (SSN) identifies the user application layer that resides above SCCP in the protocol stack.

Two basic types of addresses are discerned by SCRC: (a) a global title (GT), and (b) a point code (PC) and the subsystem number (SSN). The SCRC performs address translation for (a) its upper layer user application, such as ISUP, and (b) its lower layer MTP 3, which has received a signal unit from a remote signaling point, and needs SCRC to do some translation(s).

If SCRC receives traffic from its user layer it may receive one of the following forms: (a) destination point code (DPC), (b) DPC + (SSN or GT or both), (c) GT, or (d) GT + SSN. If SCRC does not receive a DPC from the user layer, it must derive one from (typically), the GT passed to it by the application. The derivation is usually through a mapping table that has been provisioned by the SS7 network craftspeople.

Table B–1   SCCP Addresses and Other Identifiers

Field	Contents in SCCP Message Field
Address Indicator	Flag to indicate if address has a SSN
	Flag to indicate if address has an SPC
	Flags to indicate if address has Global title
	Flag (routing indicator flag) to indicate which part of address is to be used for routing
	Flag to indicate a national or international address
SSN	One of these entries: Reserved, ISDN user part (ISUP), SCCP management, MAP, HLR, VLR, EIR, AC, spares, or not used (don't pass to user application)
Address	SSN, SPC (network, cluster, cluster member, Global title (GT) [see next])
Global Title	One of these entries: Reserved, ISDN/telephony plan (E.164/E.163), X.121 address, Telex address (F.69), Maritime numbering plan (E.210, E.211), Land mobile numbering plan (E.212), ISDN/Mobile numbering plan (E.214), see next
Digits	Digits of the Global title plan

If the SCRC receives traffic from its MTP 3 layer, this means the DPC in the MTP 3 routing label is the signalling point of this SCRC, and not the destination signalling point. It also means the originator of the traffic may want an address translation. The SCRC examines the address indicator field in the incoming signal unit. One of the bits in this field, called the routing indicator field, is set to indicate (a) that routing is to be performed based on the GT in the SCCP called party address field, or (b) routing is to be performed based on the DPC in the MTP 3 routing label, and the subsystem number in the SCCP called party address.

If case (a) is to be carried-out, SCRC must use the GT value in the called address to find the relevant DPC and SSN in a mapping table. It passes the DPC to MTP 3, which places this value in the DPC field of the routing label. The signal unit is then relayed to the next signaling point.

TRANSACTION CAPABILITIES APPLICATION PART (TCAP) OPERATIONS

The transaction capabilities application part (TCAP) is used to transfer information between SS7 nodes that are used to administer the network or support services. As a general practice, TCAP runs between the SSPs and SCPs, principally for the support of database access. As examples, the applications in the SSPs use TCAP for 800, 900, user profile operations, etc.

TCAP operates at the application layer of the OSI model but it may also include other lower layer protocols needed to support it. It operates on top of SCCP. Perhaps the best way to think of TCAP is that it is a connectionless remote procedure call (RPC) and parts of it are quite similar to the remote operations service element (ROSE) published in ITU's X.219 and X.229.

TCAP is divided into two sublayers. The transaction sublayer has services that are somewhat similar to the OSI commitment-concurrency-recovery (CCR) protocol and is organized around two types of dialogues that take place between peer entities in two machines operating in the transaction sublayer. The first dialogue is called the unstructured dialogue and is so named because no association is established between the users of this service. Additionally, no responses are provided from the receiver of this type of traffic.

The second type of dialogue is the structured dialogue and requires the retention of information about the ongoing communications between the two transaction sublayers. A dialogue identifier is associated with each message pertaining to a specific dialogue.

TACP is modeled closely from ROSE and allows an entity to issue invoke operations and return results about what happened at the machine in which the invoke operation occurred. TCAP is also employed in the intelligent network, in a manner just described.

Appendix **C**

Presentation Layer Basics

FUNCTIONS OF PRESENTATION LAYER

Intelligent networks that are defined in the ITU-T and Bellcore standards require the use of the OSI (Open Systems Interconnection) Model at the upper layers. The principal requirement is the use of the application and presentation layers. Therefore, it will be helpful for you to read this material if you are not familiar with the subject matter.

The purpose of the presentation layer is to negotiate and support the presentation aspects (syntax) of the traffic that is exchanged between user applications. Presentation layer systems provide the following services:

- Informing an application about the type of syntax that is to be used during a session connection with another application
- Imposing a structure on the syntax of the user application data
- Providing a convention encode and decode traffic in a standardized format

The presentation layer is concerned with the representation of the data in a data communications system. It provides a means to define how the bits are structured within PDUs and within the fields in the PDUs. As a simple example, it could define if the bits are positioned in a field in high or low order. It also allows two end users in two different machines to negotiate the type of syntax that will be used between two applications. For example, one user might use ASCII and the other user might use EBCDIC code. The presentation layer allows these two users to negotiate how the data will be represented, and it also supports the conversion of the data in a syntax that is acceptable to both programs.

The presentation layer uses ASN.1 (Abstract Syntax Notation 1) to define the types of data, such as integer, real, octet, bit string, and so on. It also employs a standard (X.209) to define the structure of the data for the communications channel.

PRESENTATION LAYER STANDARDS

The ISO and ITU-T have developed a presentation and transfer syntax to be used by application layer protocols (which includes the OSI network management standards). The ISO standard is ISO 8824, which is titled Abstract Syntax Notation One (ASN.1). In addition, ISO 8825 (with the Basic Encoding Rules [BER]) provides a set of rules to develop an unambiguous, bit-level description of data. That is to say, it specifies the representation of the data during the communications transfer process. In summary, ASN.1 describes an abstract syntax for data types and values, and BER describes the actual representation of the data. Figure C-1 provides a summary of these ideas.

- ASN.1 <u>defines the managed objects</u> (data), without concern for machine-dependent syntax and structures
  - Type
  - Value (possibly)
  - Name

- Transfer Syntax <u>defines bit sequences and structure of the protocol data units</u> exchanged by a management protocol
  - Type
  - Length
  - Value

- Why all these conventions?
    To eliminate "closed systems" solutions

Figure C-1 ASN.1 and transfer syntax.

Be aware that ASN.1 is not an abstract syntax unto itself, but a language for describing abstract syntaxes. Some people use the term ASN.1 to include an abstract syntax and the basic encoding rules for a transfer syntax. However, we shall see that the two are different from each other.

As a final point to this introduction, it is noteworthy to state that ASN.1 is used only in the upper three layers of the OSI Model, but it need not be restricted to these layers. It can be used at the lower layers as well, but it is unlikely that the current standards will be reissued to accommodate ASN.1. Notwithstanding, OSI now describes all data units in the upper layers in abstract syntax, and the Internet documents also use ASN.1-type notations.

ASN.1 "TYPES"

ASN.1 defines a number of "built-in" types (see Figure C–2). This term means that certain types are considered an essential part of the ASN.1 standard. They are, in a sense, predefined. They are called built-in because they are defined within the standard itself.

Boolean	Identifies logical data (true or false conditions)
Integer	Identifies signed whole numbers (cardinal numbers)
Bit string	Identifies binary data (ordered sequence of 1s and 0s)
Octet string	Identifies text or data that can be described as a sequence of octets (bytes)
Null	A simple type consisting of a single value
Sequence	A structured type, defined by referencing an ordered list of various types
Sequence of	A structured type, defined by referencing a single type where each value in the type is an ordered list
Set	A structured type, similar to the Sequence type except that Set is defined by referencing an unordered list of types that allows data to be in any order
Set of	A structured type, similar to Sequence type except that Set of is defined by referencing an unordered list of types that allows data to be sent in any order
Choice	Models a data type chosen from a collection of alternative types that allows data structure to hold more than one type
Selection	Models available whose type is that of some alternatives of previously defined Choice
Tagged	Models a new type from an existing type but with different identifier
Any	Models data whose type is unrestricted and can be used with any valid type
Object Identifier	A distinguishable value associated with an object, or a group of objects, like alibiary of rules, syntaxes, etc.
Character String	Models strings of characters for some defined character set
Enumerated	A simple type; its values are given distinct identifiers as part of the type notation
Real	Models real values (for example: $M * B^e$, where M = the mantissa, B = the base, and e = the exponent)
Encrypted	A type whose value is a result of encrypting another type

Figure C–2   Built-in types (other types are also defined).

One might wonder what is a "non-built-in" type. That kind of type is not defined in the standard and is considered to be a type that is defined by an enterprise. For example, in the Internet (as published by the Internet Activities Board [IAB]) a non-built-in type is a network address. This type is always identified as a 32-bit Internet Protocol (IP) address, in which the type must be coded as either network address.host address or network address.subnetwork address.host address.

The ASN.1 built-in types offer a wide array of types for the enterprise to use. Indeed, many organizations (in order to reduce the complexity of the presentation layer) choose to implement a subset of the built-in types.

ASN.1 RULES

ASN.1 tags (values) are assigned to each object. Each object belongs to a class (and a class number).

Presently, four classes are defined in the standard:

- Universal is a class for the built-in types
- Application is a class for a widely used OSI application (but not universal)
- Private is a class for an enterprise-specific tag
- Context specific is a class that is used to tag objects in accordance with the ASN.1 code

Types may be (1) simple (one type), (2) more complex (constructed or a "group" of types), and (3) other is not defined.

Like any language, ASN.1 has coding rules. Figure C–3 provides a brief summary of the major rules of ASN.1.

A comment is in order about the case-sensitive aspects of ASN.1. Case sensitivity is determined by coded notation in one of these three forms:

- A coded notation begins with an upper case letter: ASN.1 requires this notation to be given a type value (Integer, Boolean, etc.).
- A coded notation is "all caps": An ASN.1 reserved word.
- A coded notation begins with a lower case letter: This notation is not acted upon by the ASN.1 compiler. It is used to enhance the readability of the code.

Rules
- Character set:

    A to Z, atoz

    0 to 9

    : = , {} . () - ' " <

- Case sensative
- Layout is free format
- Comments start with "--" and end with either "—" or the end of a line

Reserved Words

BOOLEAN	INTEGER	BIT	STRING
OCTET	NULL	SEQUENCE	OF
SET	IMPLICIT	CHOICE	ANY
EXTENAL	OBJECT	IDENTIFIER	OPTIONAL
DEFAULT	COMPONENTW	TRUE	FALSE
BEGIN	END		

Figure C–3   ASN.1 rules and reserved rules.

TRANSFER SYNTAX

The use of ASN.1 by itself is not useful from the standpoint of sending traffic between two machines. Another tool is needed to describe the syntax of the traffic that is sent on the circuit between these machines. The standard used to provide this tool is a transfer syntax that is published by both ITU-T and the ISO. This transfer syntax is also known as basic encoding rules (BER). It is used to (1) describe the type of data on the channel, (2) the length of the value (in octets or bits), and (3) the data value itself (see Figure C–4).

By the use of a common transfer syntax convention, different computers can be programmed to recognize the syntax rules and correctly decode the data units.

For example, one machine might use twos complements in its architecture and another machine might use ones complement. If computer A sends traffic in twos complements representation, that traffic is so identified through the BER. The result of this operation is that computer A can translate the traffic into ones complement for use on its own internal architecture.

X.209 and ISO 8825 describe the encoding rules for the types and their values in contrast to X.208 and ISO 8824, which are concerned with the abstract description of objects. These basic encoding rules (BER) provide the conventions for the transfer syntax conventions.

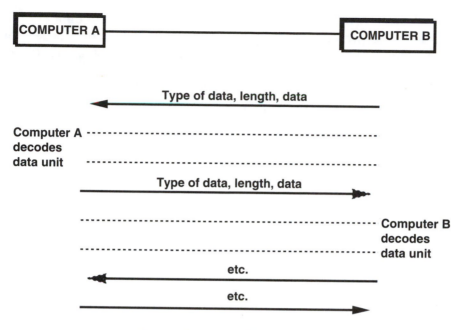

Figure C–4   The TLV approach.

The rules require that each type be described by a well-formed, specific representation. This representation is called a *data element* (or just an *element*). As shown in here, it consists of three components, type, length, and value (TLV), which appear in the following order:

Type   Length   Value

The *type* is also called the identifier. It distinguishes one type from another (for example, SEQUENCE from OBJECT IDENTIFIER) and specifies how the remainder of the element is interpreted. The length specifies the *length* of the value. The *value* (also known as contents) contains the actual information of the element, such as a distinguished name.

The length (L) specifies the length of the contents. It may take one of three forms: short, long, or indefinite. The short form is one octet long and is used when L is less than 128 octets. Bit 8 is always 0, and bits 7 through 1 indicate the length of the contents. The length value defines only the length of the contents (value) and does not include the octets that comprise the identifier and the length octets. The long form is used for a longer contents field: greater than or equal to 128 and less than 2^{1008} octets.

The contents (value) is the actual information of the element. The contents are interpreted based on the coding of the identifier (type) field. Therefore, the contents are interpreted as bit strings, octet strings, and so on.

The transfer element can consist of a single TLV or a series of data elements, described as multiple TLVs.

Appendix **D**

AIN Applied
to Toll-Free Services

This chapter describes how the Bellcore AIN is implemented for toll-free access service, and how AIN components interact with the interexchange carrier (IXC) and local exchange carrier (LEC). AIN operations are being applied to the new toll-free numbers.

REVIEW OF 800 TOLL-FREE SERVICES

In the 800 toll-free service, the 800 service access code (SAC) is dialed by the calling party to indicate the call is toll-free to the called party. The 800 number also indicates that the call must be handled differently than a conventional call, and the digits following the SAC code are used to route the call to the called party.

The 800 database contains sufficient information about the called number to determine the IXC or LEC that will carry the call. If needed, a called party number can be used instead of the 800 number for the call routing (which depends upon carrier agreements and the customer).

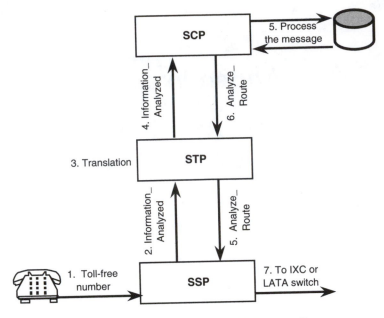

Figure D–1   An AIN toll-free call.

EXAMPLE OF AIN-SUPPORTED TOLL-FREE SERVICES

This part of the chapter contains examples of AIN-supported toll-free services. The examples are explained with an event-by-event description of the operations at the end-office, SSP, STP, and SCP.

Figure D–1 depicts the calling party dialing a toll-free number to the end office (EO). In event 1, the SSP at the EO determines that the call is AIN-related after the dialed digits are examined, which activates an AIN trigger (the trigger is the dialed public office dialing plan [PODP], reflective of new Bellcore AIN releases for toll-free service).

The SSP sends an AIN Information_Analyzed message in event 2 to a pre-determined STP pair. This message requests Global Title (GT) translation,[1] and contains field to identify the local access and transport area (LATA), a charging number, the called party identifier, and other miscellaneous information.

The SSP query message is encapsulated into a Signaling Connection Control Part (TCAP) unit data message.

---

[1]See Appendix B.

The MTP3 routing label contains the destination point code (DPC) of the STP to which the query is directed, which was obtained from the AIN trigger data. The originating point code (OPC) is the address of the SSP that creates the Information_Analyze message. The signaling link selection field is coded in accordance with usual practice.

The SSCP message fields are coded as follows:

- *Message type:* Specifies type of SSCP routing to be used for this transaction.
- *Protocol class:* Set to 0 (basic connectionless service).
- *SCCP called party address:* Contains a global title (GT) and a null subsystem number (SSN). The GT value is the dialed number (called party ID).
- *SCCP calling party address:* Contains a SSN to indicate the message was initiated by an AIN module at the originating SSP. It also contains the SS7 point code of the SSP that is to receive the response (which is the same point code as the OPC in the MTP3 routing label).

In event 3, the STP performs the GT translation on the dialed digits and, in event 4, sends the results in the Information_Analyzed message to the SCP.

The SCP receives this message. It processes it (event 5) and responds with the AIN Analyze_Route message (event 6). This message contains the routing information to process the call, which is a field in the message that identifies the carrier that is designated to handle the call. This message is relayed back to the originating SSP using conventional MTP 3 routing.

In event 7, the SP routes the call to the IXC point of presence (POP) or is processed within the LATA by the originating LEC SSP.

If the call is to be terminated with an AIN announcement, in event 6, the SCP sends a Send-to-Resource message instead of the Analyze_Route message.

The SCP response message is encapsulated into a SCCP UNIT-DATA message. This response requires no global title translation at the STP, since it is routed with the MTP3 routing label. The SSP is provided with the following information in the Analyze_Route message:

- *Routing label:* The destination point code (DPC) is the SSP that made the query (which was the point code in the calling party address in the query message). The originating point code is the responding SCP. The signaling link selection field is coded in accordance with usual practice.

- *Message type:* Specifies type of SCCP routing that is to be used for this transaction.
- *Protocol class:* Set to 0 (basic connectionless service).
- *SSCP called party address:* Contains subsystem number (SSN) of the AIN at the originating SSP.
- *SCCP calling party address:* Contains SSN of the application at the responding SCP that handled the query.
- *Transaction Capabilities Applications Part (TCAP):* Coded as an INVOKE message, the TCAP fields contain the routing information discussed earlier (the called party identifier and the carrier identification).

The Send_to_Response message may instruct the SSP to play a specific announcement because of the following conditions:

- Dialed number is an unassigned toll-free number
- Dialed number is not known
- Dialed number is to a disconnected toll-free number

Now that the SSP has the required information to route the call (the information in the Analyze_Route message), it makes the following decisions to instantiate event 7 (shown in Figure 7–1), for calls to be routed to an IXC:

- If direct trunk groups exist between the SSP and the IXC, the call is routed on the trunk group assigned to this type of traffic.
- If direct trunk groups do not exist between the SSP and the IXC, the call is routed via an access tandem (AT).
- If the direct trunk groups between the SSP and IXC are busy and an alternate routed exists through an AT, this alternate route is used.

ACCESS TANDEM (AT) SSP SUPPORT

The previous discussion brought up the role of an access tandem. In the AIN, an AT SSP acts as a hub for offices not equipped with AIN toll-free processing capabilities. The job of the end office is to recognize the AIN-related call and then seize a trunk to the AT SSP.

Since the end office does not perform the AIN operations, the AT SSP must act upon the Analyze_Route message and route the call to an IXC or within the LATA network.

Appendix E

ISDN Basics

This appendix examines layer 3 of ISDN, which is called the network layer. The intent is to provide you with sufficient information to understand the operations of the ISDN layer 3 protocol, Q.931, in the context of its relationship with the intelligent network.

PRINCIPAL FUNCTIONS OF ISDN LAYER 3

ISDN layer 3 is implemented with the ITU-T Q.931 Recommendation and other support protocols. Q.931 is responsible for setting up connections between the user station and the network, providing a limited number of support features during the connection, and terminating the connection when one of the parties in the connection issues a disconnect request (such as going on-hook). With most implementations of ISDN, the connections are mapped into the B channels, although it is also possible to send a limited amount of data traffic in the D channel when it is not being used for signalling operations.

Before proceeding further, the ISDN messages are examined. After this activity, we will analyze some examples of how ISDN establishes and manages a call between two parties.

ISDN MESSAGES

It has been emphasized that the ISDN layer 3 messages are used to manage ISDN connections on the B channels. Table E–1 lists the messages used for this purpose. The table represents the ITU-T Blue Book specification. The messages noted with an * means they have been added to the ANSI T1.607 (1990) standards. For consistency, the ITU-T specifications will be emphasized in this chapter, but I will also explain the ANSI messages.

Functions of the Messages

This section provides a description of the functions of the Q.931 messages. For ease of reference, they are listed in alphabetical order. Examples and explanations of the commonly used messages are provided later in the chapter; you might find it useful to refer to Figure 5–5 while reading about the messages.

Table E–1   ISDN Layer 3 Messages

Call Establishment Messages	*Call Disestablishment Messages*
ALERTING	DISCONNNECT
CALL PROCEEDING	RELEASE
CONGESTION CONTROL	RELEASE COMPLETE
CONNECT	RESTART*
CONNECT ACKNOWLEDGE	RESTART ACKNOWLEDGE*
PROGRESS	
SETUP	
SETUP ACKNOWLEDGE	
Call Information Phase Messages	*Miscellaneous Messages*
RESUME	CONGESTION CONTROL
RESUME ACKNOWLEDGE	FACILITY
RESUME REJECT	INFORMATION
SUSPEND	STATUS
SUSPEND ACKNOWLEDGE	STATUS ENQUIRY
SUSPEND REJECT	NOTIFY*
USER INFORMATION	

(Note: Use of these messages varies across vendors and national boundaries.)

- *ALERTING:* This message is sent to indicate that the called user party has been "alerted" and the call is being processed. This message is sent in response to an incoming SETUP message, and it is sent in the backward direction (backwards from the called end to the calling end) after the called exchange has placed ringing signals on the line to the called party.

- *CALL PROCEEDING:* This message is sent to the call initiator to indicate that the call establishment procedures have been initiated. It also indicates that all information necessary to set up the connection has been received and that any other call establishment information will not be accepted. In ISDN-conformant implementations, the CALL PROCEEDING message is exchanged only at the originating end of the connection.

- *CONGESTION CONTROL:* This message is employed only on USER INFORMATION messages. As the name implies, it is used to govern the flow of USER INFORMATION messages. In most implementations, congestion control is not used or, if it is used, it is rarely invoked.

- *CONNECT:* When the called party picks up the telephone and goes off-hook, this action precipitates the invocation of this message. The message is sent in the backward direction (from the called party to the calling party) to signal the call acceptance by the called party.

- *CONNECT ACKNOWLEDGE:* This message is sent in response to the CONNECT message. It's invocation means that the parties have been awarded the call.

- *DISCONNECT:* This message is sent when either party (calling or called) hangs up the telephone (goes on-hook). It is a trigger to the network that the end-to-end connection is to be cleared and the resources reserved for the connection are to be made available for another call.

- *INFORMATION:* As the name implies, this message is sent by either the user or the network to provide more information about a connection. For example, the message may be invoked by an exchange if it wishes to provide additional information about a connection to another exchange.

- *NOTIFY:* This message is not often used, but is available for the user or the network to provide information regarding a connection. The NOTIFY message contains a field called the notification indicator, which is described in the next section of this chapter.

- *PROGRESS:* The progress message is part of the call establishment procedure although it is not invoked in a typical implementation. However, it is available to indicate the progress of a call and it is invoked in situations where interworking is required or where the exchanges need to provide information about in-band information. This information is provided through a field in the message called the progress indicator which is described in the next section.

- *RELEASE:* This message is invoked in response to the reception of a DISCONNECT message. It is sent by the network or the user to notify its recipient that the equipment has disconnected the circuit that had been reserved for the connection. In essence, it tells the receiver that it should also release the circuit. The RELEASE message is designed also to free and make available the call reference numbers (and the associated resources) associated with the call.

- *RELEASE COMPLETE:* As the name implies, this message is sent in response to the RELEASE message and it indicates by its invocation that the sender has released the circuit, the call reference and, of course, the resources associated with the connection. The combination of the RELEASE and RELEASE COMPLETE messages means that the circuit has been completely cleared and made available for other calls, and that the call reference is no longer valid.

- *RESUME:* This message is used for a relatively simple operation, which is to request that the network resume a suspended call. The arrangements for resuming a suspended call vary between network providers, but the idea is to allow users to change their minds (within a brief period of time) upon hanging up.

- *RESUME ACKNOWLEDGE:* This message is sent by the network in response to the RESUME message. It indicates the completion of a request to RESUME a suspended call.

- *RESUME REJECT:* This message is sent by the network to indicate that it cannot fulfill the request to resume a suspended call.

- *SETUP:* The setup message contains more information elements than any of the other Q.931 messages. It is used to begin the call setup procedure. The SETUP message is always issued by the calling user to the network at the originating end and by the network to the called user at the terminating end.

- *SETUP ACKNOWLEDGE:* This message is sent in response to the SETUP message to indicate that the SETUP message has been received correctly. It is used to indicate that call establishment has been initiated. It may also indicate that additional information may be required to complete the call. For the latter case, the recipient of the SETUP ACKNOWLEDGE is required to send the additional information which is coded in an INFORMATION message.

- *STATUS:* This message is sent in response to a STATUS INQUIRY message. It may also be sent in the event of certain error conditions that occur at a network node.

- *STATUS ENQUIRY:* This message is sent by either the user or the network to inquire about the status of an ongoing operation, such as a call in progress. Both the STATUS and STAUS ENQUIRY messages are intended to be flexible enough to allow the implementor latitude in their implementation. The only information element in these messages is the display information element described later in this chapter.

  ISDN permits calls to be suspended. The reason for the suspensions are not defined in the specifications. Whatever the reasons, Q.931 provides for three messages to support these operations. They are as follows:

- *SUSPEND, SUSPEND ACKNOWLEDGE, and SUSPEND REJECT:* The SUSPEND message is sent from the user to request that the network suspend the call. The direction of the message is important in that the network is not allowed to send this message; so, call suspension can only be initiated by the user. SUSPEND ACKNOWLEDGE is an acknowledgment by the network of the reception of the SUSPEND message; it also indicates the completion of the call suspension. SUSPEND REJECT is an acknowledgment by the network of the reception of the SUSPEND message, but it indicates that the network did not suspend the call.

- *USER INFORMATION:* This message is slightly different from the INFORMATION message described earlier, in that it contains different parameters than the INFORMATION message. The major aspect is the existence of the user-user field which does not reside in the INFORMATION message. As the next section will explain, the user-user field is passed transparently by ISDN to ISDSN users.

- *FACILITY:* This message is used by either the user or the network to provide additional information about a call. Examples are keypad facility and display information, described in the next section.

- *RESTART:* This message is sent by the user or the next work to request a restart of a connection. It returns the identified channel to an idle state.
- *RESTART ACKNOWLEDGE:* This message acknowledges the RESTART message.

EXAMPLE OF A Q.931 OPERATIONS

Figure E–1 provides an example of how a call is setup with the Q.931 messages. The two persons involved in this connection are using conventional telephone handsets that are attached to ISDN terminals, shown in this figure as the calling terminal and the called terminal. The exchange termination's (ET) are located at the central offices.

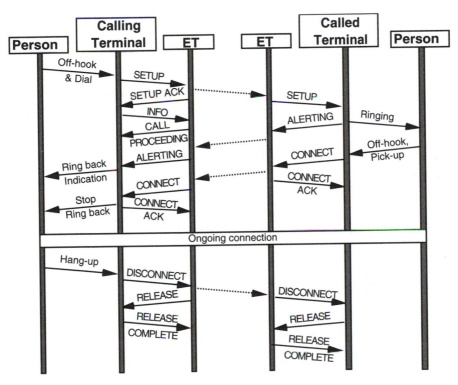

Figure E–1   Example of an ISDN connection establishment and termination.

The calling party goes off-hook and dials the telephone number of the called party. This information is used by the calling terminal to create a ISDN SETUP message, which is sent across the ISDN line to the local ET. This ET acknowledges the message with the SETUP ACK message, and initiates actions to set up a circuit to the next ET, which is shown in the figure with the dashed arrow. The SETUP ACK, and INFORMATION messages are optional, and were described in the previous section. The local ET sends a CALL PROCEEDING message to the calling terminal to indicate that the call is being processed.

At the called end, the SETUP message is forwarded to the called terminal by the terminating ET. This terminal examines the contents of the message to determine who is being called and what services are being requested. It checks the called party's line to see if it is idle, and if so, places the ringing signal on the line. When the ringing signal is placed on the line, the called terminal transmits an ALERTING message in the backwards direction, which is passed all the way to the calling terminal. This message indicates to the calling terminal that the called party has been signaled, which allows a ring back signal to be placed on the line to the calling party.

When the called party answers the call (picking up the phone and going off-hook), the called terminal sends a CONNECT message in the backwards direction, which is passed to the calling terminal. Upon receiving this message, ring back is removed from the line, and the connection is cut-through to the calling party. To complete the connection set up procedures, the CONNECT messages are acknowledged with CONNECT ACK messages.

Of course, either party can terminate the call by hanging up the telephone handset. This on-hook action initiates the ISDN connection termination operations shown in the bottom part of Figure 5–5. The DISCONNECT messages are used to indicate that the connection is to be terminated. The RELEASE and RELEASE COMPLETE messages follow the DISCONNECT messages. Afterwards, the resources that were seized for this connection are now available for another call.

Abbreviations/Acronyms

A agent
AAB Automatic alternative billing
ABD Abbreviated dialing
ACC Account card calling
ACSE Association Control Service Element
AD adjunct
AE application entity
AEIs application entity invocations
AIN advanced intelligent network
AINGR AIN Generic Requirements
AMA automatic message accounting
AMPS Advanced Mobile Phone System
AP application process
API application process invocation
APIs application programming interfaces
ASEs application service elements
ASN.1 Abstract Syntax Notation One
AT access tandem
B-ISDN broadband ISDN
BCP basic call process
BCSM basic call state model
BER Basic Encoding Rules
BRI Basic Rate Interface
BSDB Business Services Database
BT British Telecom

CCAF call control agent function
CCBS Call completion to busy subscriber
CCC Credit card calling
CCF call control function
CCF connection control function
CCIS common channel interoffice signaling
CCS common channel signaling
CD Call distribution
CF Call forwarding
CICs Carrier Identification Codes
CID call instance data
CIDFP CID field pointer
CMIP Common Management Information Protocol
CMISE Common Management Information Services Element
CMSDB Call Management Service Database
CON Conference calling
CORBA Common Object Request Broker Architecture
COT continuity message
CPR call-processing logic
CRD Call rerouting distribution
CS capability set
CS-1 Capability Set 1

CS-1/R Capability Set 1/Refined
CS-2 Capability Set 2
CT cordless telephony
DA Directory Access
DCF data communications functions
DCN data communication network
DCR Destination call routing
DDC data communications channel
DII dynamic invocation interface
DOC distributed object computing
DPC destination point code
DPs detection points
DTMF dual-tone multifrequency
EC European Community
EFs elementary functions
ET exchange termination
ETSI European Telecommunications
  Standards Institute
FEAs functional entity actions
FEs functional entities
FMD Follow-me diversion
FPH Freephone
FPLMTS future public land mobile
  telecommunications system
FSMM finite state machine modeling
GFP global functional plane
GSL global service logic
GSM global systems mobile communica-
  tion
GT global title
HLR Home Location Register
IAB Internet Activities Board
IAM Initial Address Message
IDL interface definition language
IFs information flows
IN intelligent network
INA information network and architecture
INAP Intelligent Network Application
  Protocol
INCM IN conceptual model
IP intelligent peripheral
IP Internet Protocol
IR interface repository
ISUP ISDN user part
IXC interexchange carrier
L length
LATA local access and transport area
LEC local exchange carrier

LEOs low-earth orbits
LIDB line information database
MACF multiple association control func-
  tion
MAPDUs management application proto-
  col units
MAS Mass calling
MCF message communications functions
MCI Malicious call ID
MD mediation device
MF mediation function
MIB management information base
MIT management information tree
NANP North American Numbering Plan
NAP network access point
NEF network element function
NEs network elements
OCM originating call model
OCM outgoing call management
OCS Originating call screening
ODP Open Distributed Platform
OMG object management group
OPC originating point code
ORB object request broker
OSF operations systems function
OSI Open Systems Interconnection
OSs operations systems
OSS operator services systems
PC point code
PCN personal communications network
PCS personal communications services
PDUs protocol data units
PIC point-in-call
PIN personal identification number
PMRs private modile radio networks
PODP public office dialing plan
POI point of initiation
POP point of presence
POR point of return
POS personal communications services
PRM Premium rate
QA Q adapter
QAF Q adapter function
REL Release
ROSE Remote Operations Service Ele-
  ment
RPC remote procedure call
SACF single association control function

SAO single association object
SCE service creation environment
SCEF service creation environment function
SCEP service creation environment point
SCF Selective call forwarding
SCF service control function
SCPs service control points
SDF service data function
SDL specification and description language
SDP service data point
SEC Security screening
SF service feature
SIBs service independent building blocks
SII static invocation interface
SLEE service logic environment
SLP service logic program
SLS signalling link selector
SMAE systems management application entity
SMAF service management access function
SMAP service management agent point
SMASE systems management application service element
SMF service management function
SMP service management point
SMS service management system
SN service node
SPC stored program control

SPL Split charging
SRF specialized resource function
SS7 Signaling System Number 7
SSCP service switching and control point
SSD service support data
SSF service switching function
SSN subsystem number
SSP service switching point
STP signaling transfer point
SUS suspend
TCAP transaction capabilities application part
TCM terminating call model
TCS Terminating call screening
TDP trigger detection point
TETRA TransEuropean Trunked Radio
TG Trunk Group
TMN Telecommunications Management Network
TNA telecommunication networking architecture
UAN Universal access number
UDR User-defined routing
UMTS Universal Mobile Telecommunications System
UPT Universal personal telecomm
VLR Visitor Location Register
VOT Televoting
VPNs Virtual private networks
WS workstation
WSF workstation function

Index